How to Read an Egg

Divination for the Easily Bored

How to Read an Egg

Divination for the Easily Bored

Colette Brown

Winchester, UK
Washington, USA

First published by Dodona Books, 2014
Dodona Books is an imprint of John Hunt Publishing Ltd., Laurel House, Station Approach,
Alresford, Hants, SO24 9JH, UK
office1@jhpbooks.net
www.johnhuntpublishing.com
www.dodona-books.com

For distributor details and how to order please visit the 'Ordering' section on our website.

Text copyright: Colette Brown 2013

ISBN: 978 1 78099 839 8

A CIP catalogue record for this book is available from the British Library.

Design: Stuart Davies
www.stuartdaviesart.com

Printed and bound by CPI Group (UK) Ltd, Croydon, CR0 4YY

We operate a distinctive and ethical publishing philosophy in all
areas of our business, from our global network of authors to
production and worldwide distribution.

CONTENTS

For Jim, my darling husband who makes life complete.
For my daughters, Jennifer and Jillian who continue to
thrill me and make me proud every day!

You have tried the tarot, ruminated with the runes and are all angel carded out! Now try the less well known, the tribal, the forgotten and the truly bonkers! Divination, the art of prediction or psychic insight by use of supernatural means, can be accurate *and* fun!

Introduction

I am a professional clairvoyant and tarot reader and have enjoyed using many different forms of divination in my professional life. These seem to come to me rather than me searching them out. I had always been interested in the tarot and it was always the backbone of my readings, but when I first started out professionally, I had a paperweight that had Celtic knot work designs inscribed into it and every way I turned it I saw symbols that could be interpreted for the client. I never actually wrote down a system of how this worked, but basically it was a bit like reading a crystal ball with wavy lines in it! I became quite well known as the clairvoyant who read the 'Celtic Crystal' but I did find it tiring on the eyes. Then the Runes presented themselves and I learned as much as I could about them and incorporated them into the readings as well. Along the way, there were also divinatory relationships with Psycards, ribbons, pendulums, shamanic totem cards and other oracles. However, I have been very focused on the tarot and have even had two tarot books published. The tarot speaks to me! Its wonderful visuals captivate my third eye and give me answers from deep in my psyche. I actually use three tarot decks in every reading and also use the runes to pin down dates and times. My reading desk is quite busy! I do the same sort of reading that I have done for about 17 years. It works, I am happy with it and clients come back for more.

I believe that as clairvoyant I can see and predict without anything other than my third eye. However I do feel that a divinatory 'tool' can help back up what you are receiving, make it more accurate or simply give expanded access to a question or problem. I am sure a plumber could unblock your toilet without his toolkit but it might take longer and not be so pleasant an experience. Consequently, I feel that as a clairvoyant it is important to have a toolkit too. This is where divinatory tools, such as the tarot and runes, come in very handy. I could certainly do a reading without them but I don't know if I would want to. They give me focus, extra information and look good. I feel that the client trusts the answer more if they can see that it is coming from somewhere and not simply out of apparent thin air.

Recently I was at lunch with a new business client and wasn't officially working. However, in the course of the meeting something important came up that he wanted an answer about. I didn't have my tarot cards with me (conscious decision: I am not working, just networking). I answered the question clairvoyantly and was very happy with my answer as it felt right and the client was happy. Then I panicked as I felt I hadn't had my divinatory tool with me. I realized that I had actually used a focus to help me with my answer! I had looked quickly for a symbol in front of me and saw it very clearly in my lunch! Divination by Croque Monsieur! Not that I mentioned this to the client.

This then got me thinking about how divination was done in the days before tarot cards and so forth. I also remembered that my mum had told me that when she was a young woman she used to have her 'fortune' told by an old lady who read an egg. Basically, you would take an egg from home and sit with it in your hand until you were called. The lady would then break it into water and tell you what she saw for you. I had run a psychic development circle many years ago where we tried things like tea leaf reading and dowsing and I had forgotten not only the fun of this, but also how accurate some of it could be. Obviously this was dependent on the reader.

I felt it was time to revisit a time of past experimentation and also time to explore different forms of divination again. So, I decided to look at the ancient, the 'maybe soon to be forgotten,' the unusual, the taboo and the simply weird and bonkers! I would also endeavor to gather what was necessary to do some short readings with some weirder skills of divination with willing guinea pigs chosen from my Facebook page. I would also revisit my own experiences from the past when I actually used less well-known methods.

What followed was a journey into some very weird experiences, which was at times frustrating, but which was also enlightening and truly wonderful and sometimes just very absurd! All clients' names have been changed but they are real people. I have been totally honest about the success or failure of my attempts and also about difficulties and embarrassments. I hope my experiences can help you choose a divination tool that suits you or more simply, that you become more open to challenging yourself and trying new things. Who knows...you could be the next big name in buttock reading!

Chapter 1

The Fancy 'Mancies'

Most forms of divination end in the suffix 'mancy.' I didn't realize that there were so many 'mancies' out there until I started to research. Some also have the suffix 'graphy' and some are hard to contemplate and even harder to pronounce! I had used a Croque Monsieur to help me back up a clairvoyant decision and had thought this odd. No! Food is in fact one of the most common 'mancies' out there. I felt instinctively drawn to oinomancy, the divinatory use of wine. That sounded such a good way to combine two obsessions, wine and divination, and nothing would go to waste! Yet, cromniomancy, using onions, didn't quite appeal. Ovomancy, using eggs, was a definite after my mum's stories and maybe even pessomancy, using beans. Tasseography or tea leaf reading seemed like fun and I had actually done this many years ago but stopped as most folk didn't like cold, black tea and it was very messy with lots of washing up afterwards. So food divination definitely looked like something I wanted to explore.

But even better was divination using the body. Did you know that omphalomancy is the study of navels? Talk about navel gazing! Phrenology is the use of bumps on the head and moleosophy is the study of moles to give divinatory advice. The best one has to be gastromancy, or the sounds that the belly makes! I wasn't up for spatulamancy, which involves skin, bone or poo! And to be truthful, I don't like feet so podomancy was never going to happen! Using physiognomy or facial features could be fun but may be a bit disconcerting for the client who doesn't like being stared at. Not any more so though than rumpology where their bottoms would be on show. Funnily enough, I quite fancied a go at that one! If Sylvester Stallone's mum could do it, then why not me? There seemed to be safer ground using scrying or gazing at a reflective surface and psephomancy, which used marked or indented pebbles or stones. Gazing at earth and sand as in geomancy sounded fun too as did pyromancy or reading the meaning in fire.

I was also desperate to try bibliomancy, which is asking a question, opening a book and reading a sentence or word to give an answer. Although...what books to use? There may be very different answers using the Bible opposed to *Fifty Shades of Grey*! The mad dancer in me was thrilled to hear of gyromancy, where you whirl around until you are dizzy and then interpret where and how you fall. Combining this with oinomancy, the use of wine, looked even better! The list was endless but I was going to try to choose a few and take myself out of my tarot comfort zone.

Chapter 2

Food

How to Read an Egg (Ovomancy or oomancy)

My old mum had told me, many years ago, about how she went to a 'fortune teller' in Glasgow with a group of girl friends and they all had to take a fresh egg with them. There was much hilarity and nervousness among them and they received quite a few similar readings, for instance, most would marry a tall man and have two children. This may have been more to do with the clairvoyant's ability than the particular type of reading. But I am used to the accuracy of the tarot and wondered if there could be similar by just reading the symbolism in an egg white floating in water.

I actually have had a shamanic healing and cleansing done using eggs. It was by a very trusted friend, a shaman, who wished to help me with gynecological problems. I bought six organic eggs and in the ceremony the eggs were held against various areas in my pelvic region. The shaman then sucked on the top of the eggs to pull any negativity or disease into them. The eggs were then cracked into a bowl and two out of the six had black specks of matter in the yolks. The shaman was happy with his work. I did actually feel less pain in the weeks that followed. I was the only person who had handled the eggs beforehand and therefore was sure that none could have been tampered with.

This is very like the Nordic form of using eggs for checking if a person has been cursed or exposed to the evil eye. After being left either under their bed or on an altar for a night, the egg is rolled over the body and then cracked into a bowl The egg is then examined for telltale signs of darkness or evil.

Using eggs to tell of curses or to pinpoint disease is the subject of much ridicule and articles about suspect or fraudulent shamans. Eggs can be switched through sleight of hand and replaced with previously tampered ones containing blood, meat and even small bones. In some cultures this can be accepted as simply part of the shaman's art, for instance, the performance aspect that helps the subject become more convinced of their healing. My healing was real and actually did help. I trust my friend enough to believe he was not tricking me. Plus the results were not extreme as the eggs had globules of black in them, not big whopping bits of blood and so forth.

It was time for me to try reading an egg for a client. I had decided that I would ask them to focus on a question rather than do a general reading. But first I had to find a large glass or a clear bowl. The largest glass in my cupboard had a huge red 'T' printed on it by the brewery involved and I deemed it simply not professional enough. Other glasses were too small. Help came in the form of a lovely glass bowl that held my personal crystals. It would be filled with some water and the yolk of the egg would be separated from the white, which would be poured into the water for me to 'see' symbols in. This is called hydromancy, when you look at how things are affected by water.

The Reading

I set up with my glass bowl with room temperature water in it, a pin, a tea towel and some hand wipes...just in case the egg was temperamental!

The inquirer, Helen, came in holding her egg and I asked her to concentrate on her question. She asked, 'How can I be consistently positive in the next six months at a very important time in my life?'

I took the egg and pierced it with the pin and held it over the water. And waited. The egg white didn't really want to come out of the eggshell. I shook it a bit and said encouraging words. Then I decided to make the hole a bit bigger. That helped and the egg white slowly oozed into the bowl. At first the egg white was quite clear and it was very hard to see much in it. But I think the room temperature water heated it a bit and suddenly shapes began to become apparent.

First there was a cloud and beside it, a small person. Helen is a small person who sometimes has 'clouds' of negativity around her. Then I saw what looked like shoulders and arms and felt instinctively that is represented a hug. Maybe she needed more reassurance from someone around her. Then there was a heart shape and an angry face beside it. I read this as meaning that she needed to deal with her anger about someone that was blocking her happiness, or clear past anger in her heart.

The next symbol surprised me as there was clearly another face but one of the eyes seemed to be winking open and shut! A winking face? Maybe Helen needs to learn not to take life so seriously. Then I saw teardrop formation sitting close by what looked like a ribbon with a knot in it. I took this to mean for Helen not to tie herself up in knots and also to let tears flow when necessary.

One of the most amazing symbols was when viewed from the side. There were clearly two small hands with fingers reaching upwards! I took this to mean that Helen needed to reach out more for help and understanding and maybe not be so much of a perfectionist!

The last symbol I saw was what looked liked Neptune's trident. Maybe Helen should consider a visit to the sea or time at the seaside to help cheer her up and cleanse her negative energies.

It was quite amazing how my eyes attuned to the symbols once I had started. I looked down into the bowl initially but then looked side on too. This gave a sense of three dimensions and most symbols became clearer.

I was quite happy with the symbolism that showed, although it did seem a bit general but then the question was general too.

Helen was pleased with the advice and said a lot of it resonated with her. It was all a bit fiddly and messy to be truthful. If I were to do an egg reading again, I feel I would make the water a bit warmer so that the white of the egg would maybe show up more and I also would have more practice at actually separating the white of the egg from the yolk.

In Your Cups

Tasseomancy is the art of divination using a cup. It is more traditionally associated with tea leaf reading but really can be used for anything that leaves dregs in a cup or rounded bowl. Cafeomancy is the preferred name for the reading of coffee grains and has been practiced in the Middle East for centuries. Mediterranean societies have a tradition of reading the dregs left by red wine in a glass. This is called oinomancy or oenomancy. I haven't tried oenomacy before, which is a bit silly as I consume lots of red wine. I think I will try it tonight just for myself since I have a nice Shiraz sitting beside me as I write. Well, it is Saturday!

I have had a few tea leaf readings done in the past mainly by older clairvoyants who were down to earth and had great characters. It was very common in Scotland last century for working class women to gather to read tea leaves for one another or for the fortune teller of the village or tenement building to offer this art. I have used tea leaf reading myself in more fun nights for charity and also have taught it as part of my psychic development circle. But it has been a few years since I have done it and was looking forward to revisiting this art which is in danger of being lost. Just like the shoe cobbler or the clothes mender, times have changed and some old skills are being eaten up by new technologies or trends.

I would never do tea leaf reading as part of my clairvoyant practice as it does seem quite old-fashioned and can be messy and surrounded with superstition and old rules. Yet I had found that I saw symbols easily in tea leaf dregs and felt maybe it was a cultural thing. Then I discovered that my granny on my dad's side, who lived in a tenement in Glasgow, had been known for her aptitude in teacup reading. This made me happy as I had never known her and never really knew where my psychic ability came from although I suspected it was my dad's side as he never really talked about it and was quite scared of it.

There are a few methods of tea leaf reading and many, many symbols. Traditional readers have symbols that are just used for this type of reading and frown on anyone using general symbols. If you decide to use this method often it may be wise to seek out a more specific book. I tend to think that a symbol is a symbol and has basic meanings and also personal meanings that can be used accurately by a good reader in any circumstances.

There are some amazing teacups and saucers designed and made for tea leaf reading and marked into sections and even have astrological markings on them. They can be bought online or in New Age shops. I prefer the old-fashioned way with a white cup and saucer with no patterns. You will need a teapot and real tea is necessary, not tea bags as they contain tea which is too finely cut to produce solid enough patterns when left on the cup.

The kettle is boiled and cooled slightly and poured into a big warmed pot. One heaped teaspoonful of tea is added for each person who will be read for and 'one for the pot.' The leaves are stirred and allowed to brew. Tea is poured into the cup without straining and no sugar or milk is added. The enquirer should sit sipping their tea and focusing on their question or worry. When most of the tea has been drunk the enquirer holds the cup and swirls it clockwise three times and then turns it out onto the saucer. The remaining fluid will drop and the leaves will be left stuck to the sides and bottom of the cup.

Coffee grain reading needs to be done with either a method that allows grains to be left in the brew or you can add a few grains to the coffee cup once it has been poured. The same procedure is then followed. In some traditional coffee readings the enquirer is asked to open their heart by placing their right thumb on the bottom of the cup and twisting it slightly. This mark is then seen as an indication of their underlying emotional state and interpreted using symbolism. Wine is simply drunk while focusing on the question and the sediment read once it has dried a bit.

There are a few ways to read a teacup but one of the most prevalent is for a general reading that maps out the future. The handle of the cup is held towards the enquirer and the left hand side of it represents the past and the right hand side, the future. Looking down, leaves on the rim represent a near event either in the past or future depending on what side, the middle is something further away in both directions and the bottom is seen as what misfortunes are relevant again in either past or future.

I prefer a method that answers a question or enquirer's worry. In this way, the cup isn't divided into past or future. Simply, leaves at the rim represent the present, the middle is the near future (about a month), and the bottom is the further future or potential outcome. In this way you can track symbols and also see how they change over time.

In both ways of reading, tea leaf stalks represent people with the longer stalks being male and smaller stalks being female. Crossed stalks mean arguments between people. All readers have their own interpretations, but before the tea is drunk, if the fluid bubbles, then it is seen as lucky and that money will come. Crossed teaspoons on a table or saucer indicate hearing of twins being born! Settle down and let the tea leaves become obvious to you. Some will be immediate but other will be seen as you turn the cup or tune in more. Enjoy!

The teacup reading
Alexis, a rather pretty and intelligent woman, wanted to know if her long-term love and she would ever be together.

Alexis was emotional and a bit tearful as she asked the question and I felt sad that with all the good things going for her that she actually had to ask this emotional question.

There were two leaf stalks on the actual rim of the cup, one small and the other larger and more robust. I took this to mean that the question was about now but also that it confirmed that the relationship has been there in the past and just wasn't a figment of her imagination. The two stalks were very close and almost inseparable. To my surprise this combination was repeated the whole way through the cup at various intervals. At one point near the rim section there was a gap between the flow of the leaves and this looked to me like a break up or 'cooling off' period, which Alexis actually confirmed was happening now. It is actually quite difficult to discern timings from the cup.

Off to the left was a separate cluster of leaves, which looked like a family but with one male stalk sitting very much outside it like an outsider or disconnected. There was also a bed symbol. I felt this was saying of her love that he 'had made his bed and better lie in it.' After the break or gap the male and female stalks were facing towards one another and tilted inwards which I felt meant a time when they would be pulled back together and able to reconnect. This had a little group on the outside though and I felt that the relationship may be secluded or secretive.

There was a definite wishbone further down, which I felt would be a stroke of luck or the Fates making things all right in some way. Further down again there was a distinct arrow pointing to the bottom of the cup. It was very intense and I felt I had to look at what it was pointing to. Right at the bottom were the two stalks again on a calm horizon of tea leaves. I took it that this meant to be that they had to go forward and at some point in the future they would be together as a couple and heading towards a distant horizon, which was both calm and settled.

So, the answer to the question was yes, they would be together as a couple but this would be after major transition that was purely in the hands of the Fates. The fact that the two stalks were constantly journeying together made me feel that these two were soul mates who really needed to be together but because of circumstances at the present and near future, simply could not be.

The reading itself was quite hard. The tea leaves are quite small and you really need to be very relaxed and almost not look for symbols. I was happy with the symbols I saw but I felt unsure of timings and because of this wasn't as happy as I would have been with a tarot reading where I map out the time ahead in months and years. This could be changed though if I became more familiar with the dimensions of the cup and practiced more. Still, not really for me! I felt slightly disconnected from the client as I stared hopefully into the cup and it certainly didn't allow me the visual stimulation of the tarot cards.

Alexis's response

Before the tea leaf reading I didn't really know what to expect from it as usually it's always tarot card readings I have had done in the past. I remember having a tea leaf reading a good number of years ago from an elderly lady and it was a very general reading and really no specifics or details given to me and maybe this was how I thought this reading would be.

I was pleasantly surprised when asked if I had a question I would like to ask and then to think of the question whilst drinking my tea. This made me realize that maybe it wouldn't be a general non-specific reading after all. I was glad of this as I did have a burning question I wanted to ask about my love life that had been affecting my day-to-day life and was making me miserable and felt as if I needed some guidance at this time. When Colette started to read the leaves she made comments on symbols she could see and how this could relate to the situation I am in now and what's to come. It was comforting to be told that the two leaves, which symbolized me and the man I was asking about, were staying together throughout the teacup and she was right that there was a break at the beginning as I have been separated from him for almost four months. She was correct with the comment she made when she saw the bed, "I've made my bed and now I will have to lie in it" as the man in question is very much of that attitude.

It gave me hope that one day we will be together and just to carry on the way I am until the Fates intervene.

Comparing the tea leaf reading to the tarot reading I have to say that I do prefer the tarot reading. The reason being is that the tarot is more visual and I can see from the cards that they relate to the question being asked. With the tea leaf reading you can't see what the reader is seeing and I didn't feel as involved as I would with the tarot reading. I definitely think I prefer tarot reading but was very glad to take part and experience something different.

The red wine reading

My Shiraz wine was lovely and I left just enough in the glass to see symbols in the dregs when they dried. The answer to my oenomancy question 'Has the sad decision I made recently about my lifestyle and health limitations been a good one?'

The dregs at the bottom of my glass have formed small but very clear shapes. There is a definite Ohm symbol sitting beside a very scary scorpion! Higher up there is a shark with fins. There is also a smiling face. Some of these symbols look scary but actually have good divinatory meanings. The scorpion is about self-preservation and the Ohm is symbol of sacredness. This means that my decision has indeed helped with my longer-term health preservation and also my spiritual health. This pleases me because my physical limitations were beginning to affect my spiritual happiness. The shark in the middle with the smiley face shows that in the near future I will be happier and feel that I have survived a negative period as shark means survival and the smiley face speaks for itself. So I am happy with my wine reading and slightly tipsy too!

Fruit and Nutcases!

Apples have long been associated with fertility, youth, love and temptation. If you cut an apple sideways you will see the shape of a five sided star or pentacle, which is seen as the symbol of the Goddess. Eve tempted Adam with an apple in the Garden of Eden. The apple was symbolic of sexual freedom and knowledge.

In Norse mythology the Apples of Idun hold the magic that keeps the gods and goddesses from aging. The goddess Idun is a fertility and youth goddess who grows and protects the magical apples. Freya, the goddess of love, is frequently pictured holding golden apples or surrounded by them. She is youthful, fertile and beautiful. Pomona, the Roman goddess of apples is known for her fertility and sexual prowess and lustiness. The golden apple of Hesperides sparked a contest between three Greek goddesses as to who was the fairest and poor Paris had to choose. This choice led to his obsession with Helen of Troy and all the catastrophes that followed. There wouldn't have been a Trojan horse without the apples! Who would have thought that a common fruit could hold so much magical power?

Divination with apples can be done by using the peel or the seeds. If a young woman stands at midnight, brushes her hair in front of a mirror and eats an apple to the core, she should throw it over her left shoulder. Then it is said that the face of her potential partner will appear in the mirror. You can also peel an apple in one strip and throw the peel on the floor or into a bowl of water. The shape of the peel will give the initial of your lover to come.

You can use the seeds to help choose between two suitors by taking two wet seeds, naming them and sticking them to either cheek on your face. The first one to fall off would be the one who wouldn't go the distance! The one that stays stuck would be a good long-term choice. These rituals are traditionally performed at Samhain, or Halloween, but can be done at any time if you are truly desperate.

I have also heard that if you have more than two suitors, you can write the name of each suitor on the apples while asking if they would be good long-term partners. Put them in a dark place that is kept a secret and check on them every day. The one that rots last will be the best choice. This may be quite smelly but may tell a lot about a suitor if, for example, you get a maggot growing in a rotting apple!

Oranges are considered a lucky fruit by the Chinese. They are linked with money, prosperity and love. To find out a yes/no answer to a question, eat an orange and put the seeds in front of you. An even number of seeds is 'No' and an uneven number is 'Yes.'

Nuts are plentiful and have been used for centuries for divination. Hazelnuts are roasted on a pan and if they crackle and jump it can mean that romance and passion is on its way. A newly in love couple can name two nuts and put them side by side in a roasting pan. How the nuts roast can be seen as indicative of how their relationship will progress. If the nuts roast gently and quietly, then there will be placid harmony, but if they spit and split, then why bother? Don't marry a cracked nut!

Cromniomancy or divination with onions can be seen in many countries' folklore. Okay, I know an onion isn't a fruit or nut, but my headline 'Fruit and Nutcases' wouldn't looks as good as 'Fruit and Nutcases and Onions!' And I have nowhere else to put it.

The onion is seen as a kind of cosmic representation of the Universe and life mainly because of its many layers. However, this form of divination seems more popular in Germanic countries where it has been used for many years to predict weather for the year ahead. Basically, twelve onions are chosen to represent each month of the year ahead. They are cut and several layers torn off giving cup-like shapes. A pinch of salt is laid on top of each 'cup' and they are left in a darkened room with no heat, overnight. Each onion is then looked at to see how much water has formed in the onion 'shell' and this represents how much rainfall there will be each month.

A maiden can see who her true love will be by cutting suitors' initials into an onion skin and then leaving them in a darkened room. The first onion to sprout would be her new love.

So, onions have lots of divinatory uses. When using them for divination, to avoid puffy eyes due to crying, the old method of putting a clothes peg on your nose really does work!

Let Them Eat Cake!
Aleuromancy is divination using flour. Ancient Greek wise men and priests would write their words of wisdom and guidance on paper and it would be rolled into flour and baked. These 'cakes' could then be given out at gatherings and fortunes told. This is very similar to Chinese fortune cookies. I really fancy having a go at this for my next mad party! In fact, I have already used a version of this at my wedding. I gave out bridal 'favors' of Love Hearts sweeties!

Bread baked using barley was also used to judge whether someone was a liar or a thief by the Saxons. A big chunk of the bread was placed in the person's mouth without water and if they choked, they were guilty. Our modern day version could be done using dry cream crackers! The dry cream cracker game is student fun. I bet you can't eat more than three without a drink of water. Obviously, I take no blame for choking. You do this at your own risk!

In Scotland, we have a tradition where bannocks are made from oatmeal and eaten in silence while thinking of your love life. You don't drink any water, and then go to bed and you should dream of your future mate who will offer you a drink to quench your thirst. Alternately, you place the bannock under your pillow and dream of your suitor's face. There is also a Hogmanay tradition of putting charms in clootie dumplings. These huge fruit-based dumpling are baked with flour, suet, dried fruit and spices and various objects are put in to signify luck. I remember one New Year nearly choking on a sixpence and everyone cheering my luck while I thought I was dying!

Wedding cakes have magical lore associated with them too. A bride and groom should cut the wedding cake with the bride holding the knife with the groom's hand over hers. If this happens easily without slipping, then the marriage will be one of harmony with co-operation and longevity. Beware though if you are served a slice of birthday cake and it tips over before you eat it. You are not long for this world! Cake can be dangerous!

Chapter 3

The Body

Holy Moley!

The art of divination by looking at the meaning of moles on the body is called moleosophy. It is related to astrology in that the moles or birthmarks are believed to be accrued at the time of birth or of conception. Although this is occasionally seen in Greek mythology it is more commonly linked to Chinese forms of divination where moles are examined for auspicious signs, deadly warnings or common personality traits. Because of this it is often used as an adjunct to astrology charts.

A lot of lore regarding moles seems negative. Basically, it would be better to have no moles at all! There is certainly coalescence of most of the mole meanings. This tends to mean that it is a system of divination that has been used and qualified through many years. Information has been built up and can be used to help overcome a negative personality trait or to predict wealth or good luck in life.

This system of divination is based on the color, shape and area of body that the mole has presented itself. Light-colored moles are seen as auspicious and lucky but only if they aren't on unlucky parts of the body. Dark-colored moles are not very lucky even when on lucky parts of the body. (These are also probably more likely to need looked at by a doctor!) Raised moles have more power than flat ones and little ones are not as important as big ones. Hairy moles are not lucky but if the hair is short then you might just be okay, especially where money is concerned! Round moles are good. Angular shapes are not.

So first has to be the belief that moles and birthmarks have some astrological significance and that certain areas of the body have specific meanings. Yet the areas of the body didn't make much sense at all. It seemed very random. Yet most of the information was repeated time and time again just like astrological interpretations of sun signs are pretty fixed.

So first I thought I would look at my own moles. I had one dark mole on my right leg that after a silly dalliance with high-powered sun beds before a French holiday had to be cut off! Fair haired, Celtic types should really be more sun aware and possibly less vain. This mole was truly bad luck. I kind of knew this when it turned darker and crusty round the edges! I had another one on my right knee, which wasn't very pronounced but annoyed me at times. I also have a very small mole at the base of my neck. So what did these moles mean?

The mole on my throat is small so therefore doesn't carry much weight. It is very pale which can be seen as good luck. This placing indicates a successful career but with hard work paying off over time. It also indicates being very lucky with friendship and having a sense of elegance! So far so good. I have had a successful career in pharmacy, then clairvoyance and am now exploring my writing career. I have amazing friends. But elegance…nope! I do try but it just doesn't seem to work for me.

The mole on my right knee is small but raised and is a light color. This portends a happy marriage and lack of marital stress. Tell that to my divorce lawyer! Although it didn't stop me doing it again and so far, so good!

Now to the big one. The dark-colored raised mole on my right shin that went onto being a step far too near being skin cancer! Ouch…this means that I am lazy, selfish and likely to offend people. As a Taurus I am a very hard worker, pride myself on being caring and think before I speak as much as I can. So this doesn't really sound like me at all. Maybe this is what I would have been if it hadn't been sloughed off by a very kind doctor. Or maybe I would have been dead. Oops…well maybe I do offend people by speaking without thinking!

My subject for the mole reading, Gordon, was quite moley and

I photographed his torso front and back. I wondered if some of his moles would show vanity as he pulled his belly in and flexed his muscles as I took the photos but that could be just a 'man' thing! Then it was just a case of examining the photos and presenting him with the reading, which is more about personality than prediction.

The Reading

Gordon's chest area has two main moles one of which is to the left hand side of the mid line and is dark, hairy and raised but very circular and the other to the right hand side and is flat and an oblong shape. Moles on the chest area can indicate a laziness and/or prevarication: why do today when you can do it tomorrow? Both of these moles have both positive and negative meanings due to shape, hairiness and color. So maybe they mean that Gordon has the ability to cancel out some of his tendency for being too laid back with a sense of obligation or pride in achievements.

The back area has a protruding mole on the lower left shoulder, which is a very light-colored pink. Protruding moles are viewed as being very lucky, but in this area are symbols of quite a hard life with many knocks resulting in quite a resilient character. So maybe the lucky shape of the mole has given Gordon a few lucky breaks that have helped him not to define himself by trauma or loss.

Gordon has a very distinct mole on his right hip just above the buttock area. This can mean that he is generally contented in life and could be quite spiritual in his outlook and thought patterns. This mole is flat and very circular with no ragged edges. This could mean that Gordon has reached a certain time of completion and harmony in his life and maybe has come full circle in terms of spiritual beliefs.

The patterns of Gordon's moles suggest a laid back person who may need to watch out for procrastination, putting things off until they build up too much and also maybe not being as alert to challenges as he could be. Yet, the colors and placing also show a spiritual person who has pride in his achievements without being overly materialistic or driven. They also show a person who is spiritual in outlook and comfortable enough in his own skin not to be bullied into action by others.

Gordon's reply

Yeah; in a very general sense it does seem fairly accurate. However, I don't think that it can be or appears to be predictive. Certainly it could help to know something of this if you have a need to get to know someone. Though it does not appear to be too reliable. It is very astrological it seems in its basic structure, and as it appeared to give my general personality, there is nothing 'deep.' So I couldn't say that this would be a reliable form of divination. I could go so far as to say that it is not a form of divination; more in the sense of that 'science' of reading a person!

Thanks for the reading and your time.

Gordon.

I felt too that this form of divination was very general and actually was very confusing to do. It wasn't one for me, I am afraid and I wouldn't contemplate it again.

Navel Gazing

Omphalomancy is the study of navels or belly buttons! Navel gazing! The more ancient art of Umbilocomancy is used to predict the number of children a woman may have. It involves looking at the umbilical cord of the first-born child and seeing how many knots or kinks there are along its length. Each one represents a future child! I didn't think that a maternity hospital would give me access for research so I decided to try Omphalomancy and interpret some photos of belly buttons!

When I announced this on my Facebook page and asked for volunteers, the call was answered within 16 seconds! Even after I said that I had my two subjects, folk still emailed me their belly button photos. It seems more people are interested in this than I imagined. Or maybe I just have some weird Facebook friends.

According to Dr. Gerhard Reibman, a psychologist who knows about belly buttons, the shape of the navel can give much information on personality and also life expectancy. I am not sure about the life expectancy bit as so many other factors can affect that, including weight and girth rather than personality type. But I will give the clients' navels my best attention and based on information available and my intuition, I will prepare reports and ask the clients for feedback.

The things I will be looking for include whether the navel is an 'outy' or an 'inny'; whether it sits more horizontal or vertical in line or whether it is simply round. I will also be looking at whether the belly button is centered or not and anything else intriguing on the photos.

First up is Iain's photo

Iain's belly button is off center and this indicates he is a bit of a weird person with emotional swings and a diverse outlook on life. He will have broad views, support the underdog and will be very, very interested in unusual outlets for talent. He will have a great sense of humor, which might not be truly understood at times. His thinking may be 'off center' and this will make him good at jobs where he has to think outside the box.

Iain's belly button also is an 'inny' and sits slightly vertically. People with inny navels can be sensitive and gentle and have a tendency to worry too much. They also need reassurance and can be prone to jealousy and tantrums when stressed. Yet the slightly vertical nature of his navel should balance this as it represents a strong character with a sense of duty and responsibility for friends and family and co-workers. He will also stand up for a cause if the cause is right. Certainly not a wallflower!

Iain's belly is round and shaped very much like an orange…hence the name 'navel orange' I suspect. His belly seems to be proud and part of him yet I feel it serves as protection too. Having built up 'layers' in this area, he should ask himself what emotions he is protecting himself from and if that aspect of his life should be brought to the surface and worked on. An old Native American told me that 'once I had dealt with outstanding fears and emotions, the layers I kept round my belly would simply melt away.' It will be obvious to my friends that I must still not have dealt with some emotional stuff! Either that or both Iain and I just love food!

Iain's belly button therefore shows him as a man who is complex in himself, yet warm and funny with others. He would make a great partner as he has lots of love to give and is generous to a fault. But he would need to watch for jealousy and lack of self-esteem.

Iain had asked a question about his home life, whether it would resolve itself and whether he would live with someone or on his own? I don't feel that the navel reading can give this specific type of answer like, for example, tarot cards could. But based on his navel personality type I feel he would only be able to live with the completely right person. If the person wasn't a close friend or lover, his own sensitive nature might be too overpowered and he would feel overwhelmed. It would be better for Iain to live on his own until he felt totally committed to someone.

Here is Iain's reply

It's fab and very accurate. The bits that strike a definite chord with me are 'off center' and thinking outside the box. I work in a job that is about investigating internal theft issues and is about analyzing information and thinking laterally so that you can uncover scams and getting into the mind of people who are abusing the system. In fact the term thinks outside the box is on my CV.

Some years ago when I was putting together a dating profile I couldn't think of what to say about myself and my character so I asked my close friends to describe me in ten words, almost everyone used the words, sensitive, funny, worrier and complex all of which you have touched upon. All of them used the words loyal friend too, which again you touched upon. I personally would agree that I can be prone to needing too much reassurance and that lack of self-esteem is an issue for me but mostly when it comes to my relationships and hence the jealousy. As far as the 'layers' go, I have always seen myself as a person who is more comfortable expressing emotion externally rather than internally so maybe my belly is the ultimate external expression of my emotions lol. I do overeat when I am stressed however and I've always seen that as a perceived weakness so that is probably my hidden emotion that manifests itself in my big belly lol. As far as my question goes, I was thinking more about the physical space of my home (would I move etc) rather than who I would live with, however, the opportunity to share a home within a relationship has come up recently as an idea, and I have resolved that I would live on my own until I was in a committed relationship, so that too is very accurate. Many thanks for this Colette.

Iain x

Maria's photo

Maria's belly button was different. Although it was still an 'inny' it was actually very horizontal and sat squarely in the middle of her belly. So, like Iain's inny she will be sensitive and nice and actually make a great friend. She will also think deeply on issues which are close to her heart. Yet, the horizontal shape could bring her to being more nervy and prone to anxiousness than is necessary. She may question her decisions far too much and get herself in a pickle about what people think of her. This inny and line combination means she would need to watch how she reacts to the outside world and how she interprets criticism. Being highly strung and anxious could cause stress related illness and be damaging to her health if she doesn't relax more and take time off from worrying.

The saving grace is her very central belly button and slightly oblong look of her torso. This will make her a stable influence in people's lives and someone who could be counted on for good advice and hospitality. She will be methodical when she needs to be and very focused on children and the health and harmony of those she loves. She would still need to stop being so hard on herself!

Maria's question was about whether she had made the right decision in a business venture and if it would bring in decent income?

Since her venture is linked with hospitality and looking after people, I feel she has made the correct choice according to her navel personality. She will be meticulous with the business but would need to watch that she doesn't over worry or let little pieces of criticism get to her. Her strength is in her need for people to have a good time and have fun…so in this case I see her business venture doing very well.

Here is Maria's reply

Hi Colette, how you can tell all that from my belly button, lol. Everything is very accurate, I do need to learn to relax more and learn to de-stress, so happy about my wee business venture it's very exciting.

Brilliant thank you.

Maria xxx

As you can see from this feedback, the clients did enjoy their mini readings and found them accurate and enjoyable. I also enjoyed doing them but won't be giving up my tarot!

Bottoms Up!

I know you have all been waiting on this one! Rumpology: the art of divination by reading bottoms! All very 'salacious seaside postcard' and certainly not one that gives me any sense of professionalism or integrity. Yet, if there is some accuracy in palmistry, the reading of the lines on the hand, or physiognomy, face reading, then who is to say that buttock or bum reading should be any less accurate? It just feels a wee bit tacky and to be honest, there really isn't much information out there on it. Palmistry has had much written about it and explanations seem to make sense so it has gained acceptance as a form of divination. In my opinion there simply isn't enough information to give rumpology any form of weightiness or prestige in the world of divinatory tools. There are many claims that it is an ancient art practiced by Babylonians or Romans, but I couldn't actually find any proof of this.

It is very common for a person to visit, say, a tarot reader and for people not to think twice about it now. Many of my clients are business men and women who are not only very successful but very clever and respectable. They have no problem in passing on my business card to a fellow professional. Yet, I don't feel that they would view rumpology in the same way. It all seems just a bit of a joke.

The main protagonist of rumpology is Rambo's mum, Jacqueline Stallone. She promises to tell you about your personality and guide you on your future by perusing a photo of your bum. I really don't see many of my clients being willing to do this and I certainly would be suspicious if any one asked me to handle their bum/butt. Yet Ms. Stallone is protective of her art and defends it against ridicule while seeing the humor in it. Just because she has a famous son and comes over slightly bonkers at times doesn't mean that this method isn't a potential form of divination. She may well be genuinely clairvoyant and this just happens to be one of her divinatory tools. Certainly an odd and different one but it takes all sorts to make a world.

Rumpology can be done by either looking at a photo of a person's bum *or* feeling the buttock area just like you would feel the skull in phrenology. For you, dear reader, I will attempt the former but not the latter!

The interpretation of the bum is linked to the shape, marks or dimples and general fullness of the bottom. It also is based on the belief that the left buttock represents the past and the right buttock, the future. As to the gluteal line or crack, the length or straightness seems to be the key! But the key to what, I am not very sure!

I decided to do two bum readings so I could contrast and compare different shapes. The problem was that no one actually wanted to take part. Even the promise of a free reading advertised through both my Facebook pages didn't bring much success once it was explained that I would need a photo of the person's bum. Finally two brave souls, both female, agreed to take part but only if the photos were private and their names were changed. The photos duly arrived and I had the silly joy of making them full size on my PC screen. I had decided that I would look for symbols just like in any other reading or try to divine what shape and tone meant. I decided to do each person a personality reading based on the general shape etc and a past and future reading based on the symbols that were on their skin. Then I would prepare a report and ask for their feedback.

Stef's reading

After looking intensely at this bottom, I have to say that I don't feel this type of reading is for me. There isn't much info so I have had to look for symbols and kind of go mainly on instinct.

The left buttock is slightly smaller than the right, which would mean that Stef has more life ahead than she has already had if we are using it as a timeline. Also there is much more going on in the way of marks on the 'future' buttock than on the past one.

Obviously I have discounted marks that are obviously from sitting or from jeans. The past buttock seems to have two children's faces on it showing two children in her past and the future one seems to have an animal that looks like a bull. So there will maybe be a new pet or the influence of someone born under the sign of Taurus? Or maybe Stef will become more stubborn as she ages?

The past buttock has one main line on it showing maybe a straightforward path in life. But the future buttock has at least four dents showing maybe much renewal and a few changes in outlook or path in life.

The gluteal crack veers slightly to the left and this could mean Stef struggles sometimes to move away from past thought processes.

Stef's bum is toned and flat which could allude to health consciousness and she could also be a bit of a tomboy. There is fullness on the inner parts of the buttocks rather than the outer parts, which could mean Stef holds her sensuality in a private way and is not very extroverted or showy.

To be honest, this is the worst type of reading I have done and would never do it again. There is an embarrassment factor and unless the client's bum is covered in marks and thread veins which this one isn't, there isn't really a lot to work with.

I decided not to even bother with the second bum reading. I was not impressed and felt as though I was making it up as I went along. I obviously don't have Ms. Stallone's gift or knowledge for interpreting butts! I also had the embarrassment of my postman looking in my window as he was delivering the mail. This cheery chappie looks in and waves or taps the window most days. But today he blushed and walked straight to the door. I think seeing me staring intently at a full-size bottom on my PC screen has changed his opinion of me a lot!

Stef's reply

I found the past reading to be fairly accurate; I have two children and try to be healthy. I do struggle to move away from the past and am a quiet person who would rather hide at the back than be in the limelight. I am not one for dresses and make up and so agree with the tomboy remark. As for the future, we will have to wait and see.

Chapter 4

Psychometry

Feeling the Force!

Psychometry is the psychic art of obtaining information by touching or handling an object. It is linked to clairsentience, which is psychic 'feeling,' and can be used to give facts about the object through feelings, visuals or sounds. The object can hold the energy of its history or can give feelings or emotions of the person it belonged to. It can also lead to visuals or sounds of a certain important event it has been linked to or just a sense of the person and their connection to it.

The term psychometry was coined by Joseph Rodes Buchanan in the 19th century. He believed that all things emanate energy and this energy could be picked up on and used to allow us to sense emotions, events and experiences associated either with the object itself or the person or place that it is strongly connected with. It is also called object reading and psychoscopy.

Any object theoretically can be used but metal seems to hold the psychic memory better and that is why jewelry is used in many readings. But stones, crystals and cloth can work quite well too. Someone who is skilled in psychometry will be able to take an object into their hands and give a commentary of what they feel from it and this can sometimes be so accurate as to be shocking.

Although I can pick up lots of vibrations and energy from places, I have never regarded myself as very good at the art of feeling things through touch. This has annoyed me at times as I feel it can be one of the most impressive psychic skills to have and is very popular. I can be in a place and be almost overwhelmed with emotion, a sense of what happened there or even the people's stories that may have been absorbed. I have helped out in investigations of assault and theft and seen and felt things quite clearly. I have read through ribbons in the past and used a Celtic crystal, which clients have held before I tuned into it, so I must have some psychometric skills.

I think I know why I don't feel I am very good at psychometry. It comes from fear and a bad memory of being put on the spot, many, many years ago. When it became known locally that I was clairvoyant, I had a negative experience at a hairdressers, of all places. There I was, sitting with a huge rubber cap on, covered in peroxide, developing my blonde streaks, when the hairdresser took off an old antique ring and thrust it in to my hand. 'Awww I love all this spooky stuff! What do you get from my granny's ring? Tell me!' she said. My first thought was...I don't want to do this. It just didn't feel right. It felt disrespectful and in any case, I wasn't even remotely in an 'open' mood. But, as you do, when another six sets of eyes had trained themselves on me, I felt I had to try. Disaster! Nothing! Not a wee visual or so much as an emotion. I handed it back apologizing for my lack of skill. Those looks and the humiliation have stayed with me. Since then, I really haven't believed in myself as a practitioner of psychometry.

Yet, now I am older I can see that if I was now in the same situation I would handle it differently. Basically, I will not be a performing monkey for anyone! I only give advice when I am doing readings or have meditated properly and I certainly don't do it for anyone else's entertainment. My own ethical code now would prevent me even accepting an object foisted on me. I would politely decline, citing reasons of ethics and letting them know that I don't walk about 'open' all the time. I have the confidence to show the respect for my art, that I didn't have back then. This confidence came in handy just this year when I was on a hired minibus coming back from a friend's birthday celebration. It had been a great night and I was rather drunk and very exhausted. As I settled into my seat for a quick snooze during the journey, a woman came on and shouted, 'Oh! You are that scary woman! I miss my granny. Please say you have a message for me from her?' Inappropriate or what? I calmly explained that this was neither the time nor the place and that if she wanted a reading she could phone for a private sitting like anyone else. I can actually feel myself bristling as I write this. Honestly, I am not an angry person, but I feel that a lot of very professional psychic people are completely misunderstood and denigrated by some people's attitudes to the paranormal world. You wouldn't ask a lawyer to give you free advice when it was obvious they were tipsy and socializing. I would never consider asking my dentist to have a wee look at my fillings in a social situation. So, why are people who work with clairvoyance, mediumship or healing seen to be fair game? Attitudes are changing though and I hope that these misunderstandings will be a thing of the past soon.

Anyway, back to psychometry! I have always been interested in the way that objects hold memories of events or feelings and I had included teaching this as part of a psychic development course. Most of my students were as nervous as me as I handed them items of which I knew the history and some reacted to the fear by shutting down, just like my younger self. Some students gave general accounts of what they felt that were good but not that spectacular. But two students blew me away with their information.

One item was very precious to me. It was my younger child's silver bracelet, inscribed with her name, which she wore from a young age until it was too tight. I was hoping my student would be able to describe my daughter and give a sense of her personality. Yet what she sensed sent a chill down my spine. She said she immediately felt terror and fear from the bracelet. She then felt herself fall forward and crash down some stairs with a heavy weight on her and felt terrible pains in her head. She heard screaming and then sensed a hospital.

This was amazing because not long after my daughter was

given the bracelet we had some friends over for dinner and their children were playing with my older girl in her room upstairs. I had strapped my young one in her buggy in the hall to let her sleep away from the noise. My older daughter, who was five years old, unbeknown to me, decided that her wee sister who wasn't even one yet should come upstairs and play with the other kids. So she started to take the buggy upstairs and just at the top, she realized that she couldn't hold it. It was too heavy and she had to let it go or she would have fallen with it. It tipped forward and my daughter's face hit every step on the way down. The full weight of the buggy was on top of her and it was one of the worst sights of my life. After head x-rays at the hospital we were allowed to take my wee one home. She had bruises and carpet burns all over her cheeks and forehead but happily, the rest of her wasn't injured due to being strapped in her buggy. Oh, and she also was left with a fear of falling down stairs, which has never really left her.

When I told my student the facts behind her findings, she was genuinely impressed with herself. So she should have been!

The second object was a very odd one. It was an old wooden doorknob. It meant a lot to me and I had kept it since I was sixteen. When I handed it to my student, she looked at me with horror as though she had drawn the short straw. She was about to give up then suddenly she felt it held a lot of love and that she felt I had handled it a lot when I was stressed. I laughed out loud at this as she was so spot on. Then she told me she thought it was from a hospital because she saw a man in a white coat that looked like a doctor. He had lots of children around him and there was a smell of chemicals in the air. She said she felt that I removed the doorknob in a sneaky way and that I would be embarrassed by the story behind it. By this time I was in stitches but also embarrassed as I knew I would have to own up. I had hoped she would sense just where the object had come from…but no, she had the full cringeworthy story! The building was not a hospital. It was a school. The man was not a doctor. He was a chemistry teacher I fell in lust with on the first day he turned up at my all girls' convent school! He wore a white coat to lessons, the room smelled of chemicals and he was always surrounded by lots of pubescent, adoring teenage girls, the poor man! The school had to close when I was in fourth year and on the last day needing to have a reminder of my time there I sneaked into the science department with a screw driver and removed the doorknob. I needed something to remind me of my heartthrob. Never under-estimate the influence of a teacher! I went on to study pharmacy at university and was known to sit and hold a very old doorknob when I was stressed! Again, my psychic student had proved how accurate psychometry could be!

So how do you become adept at this skill? I feel you need a genuine talent first. Anyone who has a love of the feel of things will be one step ahead. Being tactile must surely help. Anyone with healing hands or who does energy work should be already quite able. If you love crystals and can feel their energy, again, psychometry may well be easy for you. It is important to be very relaxed and to have meditated. It may also be wise to wash your hands thoroughly for bacterial reasons and also to cleanse them.

Sit comfortably and let your third eye open and feel the heightened sense of feeling. Then let yourself feel your hands, which should be palm up resting on your legs or a table. At this stage you may feel a strange sensation of your palms warming up or a feeling like there are pins and needles on them. This can also just feel like a breeze wafting over them. If you have no sense of feeling coming from your hands, try holding two clear quartz crystals for five minutes in each palm. If there is still no sense of different feelings in your palms, then this psychic art may well not be for you.

Pick up an object and just let images and feelings run through your mind. If you have no one to take notes, then make sure you record yourself rather than stopping and reaching for a pen and paper. If your eyes are closed and you are really sensing things or seeing images, writing will stem the natural flow. If you are not sensing much, try holding the object on the third eye area of your forehead before you give up on it. It may just be that you don't have sentient palms and the third eye may totally tune you in.

Once you have finished, thank the object for its information and put it down. Then try again with another object. These objects should be collected from people and not your own items. It is better not to know any of the stories associated with them or you may not be sure if imagination rather than psychic ability is at play. When you are completely finished reverse your meditation, close down your third eye and have a wee listen to what you have recorded. Then compare it with what others know to be fact about the objects.

One form of psychometry I have been fine with and found easy was reading with ribbons. I know reading with ribbons can touch on color divination but I simply used them to connect with clients. I don't know what led me to this technique. It was a very long time ago and worked very simply. I know some clairvoyants ask to hold clients' hands across the table and then tune into them. I tried this but it could be uncomfortable and some people find the intrusion too much. Plus hands can get sweaty! So I found that holding a ribbon between me and the enquirer was a good way of having contact without entering someone's personal space.

I went to the local haberdashery store and bought one meter lengths of ribbons of most colors of the spectrum. I bundled them together, tied them in another loose ribbon and let them fall over the table. Once the client had settled I asked them to choose a ribbon and hold the end nearest them. Then I found the other end in my bundle and simply held it. Very soon, I could feel the person's emotions and felt real empathy for them. Flash pictures would appear in my head that I could interpret and advise on. The visions tended to be about the 'right now.' So I could have a clear understanding of the person's question. At other times I could feel and see maybe an incident or problem from the past and we could talk about that too. I didn't really focus too much on the color the person chose at all but always felt more comfortable when the person chose yellow, say, instead of black! Most people chose blue anyway and it was always the grubbiest ribbon. Ribbon psychometry works well if you are empathic and work visually so is excellent for clairvoyants like myself. Yet, it can be draining and I don't feel gives specific answers for the future but it maybe does give access to questions and problems.

If you want to work at a deeper level with ribbons I feel that you would need to understand color and know what each color symbolizes. I know some people equate color to certain chakras and therefore could use ribbons to see where the client has a blockage depending on what color is subconsciously chosen. But color can also represent a person's state of mind so I am not sure how accurate ascribing it to the chakras might be. Again I feel it would be dependent on how good the clairvoyant/healer was and how they set out to use the ribbons.

It was time to try psychometry. I wasn't very confident but was willing to try to ditch my fears and overcome my confidence issues.

Marie's reading

Marie handed me a ring and asked me what I could sense from it. I assumed it was the ring of a deceased family member (as so often rings are) but immediately had visions of a wedding and sensed the names Campbell, Joyce and Peter. Marie confirmed that these were family members who attended her wedding and that it was her own wedding ring. Note to self: dump preconceptions that jewelry offered for psychometry readings only belongs to dead people!

I felt a deep soul connection bond between her and her husband and then unexpectedly that she conceived a wee boy just after the ring was given to her. She confirmed that her son had been a honeymoon conception! Then I tuned through the ring to feelings from her son that worried me. I felt dizzy and disorientated and also that there was red bump or scar on his cheek. Maria said she had been very worried about him as a few days previously he had a sports injury that had given him concussion and he had been in hospital. He had also injured his cheek.

I then sensed Marie herself in the ring and felt that she had very unhealthy bones and would need help with osteoporosis in the future. She said that her mum suffered in this way. I also felt tummy troubles.

I also felt strange sadness thinking about her dad and then got a big shock. I heard a folk song being sung in what sounded like a Russian language. Maria laughed as her dad was Eastern European descent and was a folk singer. They were estranged and she had been thinking about him.

I then felt that she was worried about her mum and sensed quite severe pain in my eye. Marie's mum had been treated for glaucoma recently. I also felt that there was a spirit called Agnes who was worried about her. This was her mother. After this the ring seemed to close down and I felt very little so I ended the reading.

I was truly delighted with the specifics I felt from the ring and so pleased to be able to say that I could do psychometry! The information came in waves like the ring was opening a computer file, giving me the insights and then closing it again before moving onto the next stage after a wee break. I thoroughly enjoyed the reading.

Marie's response

I enjoyed the reading a lot and was surprised by its accuracy. I had expected that Colette would get one or two pieces of information but there were lots. I felt it was the same as any in depth reading. I was so pleased that the ring allowed Colette to access my son and family members as well as both past and present issues and events. I enjoyed seeing clairvoyance work without visual tools like the tarot. Colette had also told me how nervous she was about doing psychometry so I was pleased to be part of a reading that gave her confidence back.

Chapter 5

Scrying for a Vision!

Scrying is the name for divination using a reflective or shiny surface to see past, present and future. Although it is mostly associated with crystal ball reading, scrying can be done with almost anything that has a reflective surface or a sense of depth. You can scry using a deep pool of water, a bowl of water, a crystal, a mirror or even flames and smoke. This form of divination is very old and can be read about in many ancient cultures. It is associated with druids and witches in Europe and has almost a fanciful folklore about it. Snow White's evil queen had a magic mirror, which she gazed into, and many recent movies have included scrying tools like the stone used by the queen of the elves in *The Lord of the Rings*. Nostradamus was said to have used scrying for many of his predictions.

I have always found scrying quite valuable yet also quite tiring. If you haven't scryed before it is important to build up to it by meditating first and exploring your own mind and understanding your own symbolism. Otherwise you might find you are frustrated when you don't see very much at all.

Crystal balls and crystals should be transparent and also have no flaws, or very few. Some scrying mirrors are quite expensive due to the time and techniques used for making them flawless. My husband made his own scrying bowl and it took him quite a while to feel happy with it. So unless you want to spend ages painting a surface black and even, then simply invest in a scrying tool or use nature. Water in a puddle can be just as effective if you are in the right frame of mind. Ordinary mirrors can be used for scrying too but I find I can almost see too much in mirrors. Plus if I want to scry for information on events I tend to be distracted by spirit faces appearing in the mirror. My wonderful first mother-in-law seems to find mirrors a very easy way to show herself in spirit. Not good if you are sleepily brushing your teeth in the dark at night. Thank you, Mum, for the good frights!

Once you have meditated, look into the scrying bowl, crystal or mirror. Try to kind of 'unfocus' your eyes and look beyond the surface, deep into the depth and then see what is shown to you. This can be done with smoke or flames too. Some of my best scrying has been done simply sitting at my window gazing into a snow blizzard outside. Mesmerizing! I have also had the same effect when looking at the TV when it isn't tuned into the channels. All that 'white noise' can induce the trance-like state that scrying works best with.

Some people feel that scrying should only be done in the nighttime as it is under the auspices of the moon. Candles can give a wonderful eerie background glow when lit behind the enquirer. I find that scrying can be done at any time as long as the light is a bit gentle and not too strong. Direct sunlight doesn't really work.

Nature can be very helpful in scrying. Native American holy men traditionally cry for a vision during a Vision Quest ceremony. They are very well prepared for the scrying by first undergoing the rigors of sweat lodge and then the fasting and exposure to the elements required over the traditional four-day quest. There is no food or water allowed apart from maybe water, which has come naturally into the sacred circle by either rainfall or dew. The holy man is not allowed to succumb to sleep and must chant and pray to keep sleep at bay. At one point he will be so exhausted and out of it that he cries out for his vision. If he is blessed it will come. This may take the form of a hallucinatory vision in front of his eyes as he is focused on an object, the colors around him, the grass, the stream or the sky. This, to me, is the ultimate scrying experience, one that I have taken part in and will never forget. However, this is extreme and scrying can be gentler and certainly more comfortable when done using meditation, a prepared scrying tool and a big comfy chair!

You may need to look up a dictionary of symbols (some are provided at the end of this book) and also to interpret what certain symbols may mean to you. You can also back up what you have seen by asking for a tarot card or rune to confirm your thoughts or interpretation. Scrying is hard work on the eyes and also on the brain. I would say it should only be tried once you have tried some less exhausting methods of divination.

Chapter 6

Books and Lyrics

50 Shades of Enlightenment

Bibliomancy is the art of divination using books. It is sometimes called stichomancy which is more about reading lines or verses to guide on the future. This is a very ancient art. Basically, for as long as there have been books, there has been bibliomancy. How often in our daily life has something random in a book resonated with us or with a question that has been uppermost in our minds? This happens to me a lot, so I am very interested in doing some bibliomancy just for myself!

This form of divination is seen as the random selection of a verse or even phrase from a book that is accepted to be steeped in wisdom. The main one used in the Western world seems to be the Bible but Eastern texts, such as the Koran and Torah, have been used too, although some orthodox religions forbid bibliomancy as still being a form of fortune telling or linked to the occult. Some civilizations used the works of their famous poets like Homer or Virgil and chose random samples of the great odysseys.

These random selections are sometimes known as sortilege which is like drawing lots to decide what the answer is to a question. The I Ching is the most famous form of sortilege where yarrow sticks and coins are used to form a pattern, which then is explained in the pages of a book. The tarot is likened to bibliomancy as well, except the cards represent non-bound book pages.

I wanted my experience to be modern and fun and to check out different answers to questions by using different texts, some more modern than others! In fact, one of my most accurate examples of sortilege came not with the written words but with the lyrics of a song. One of my favorite songs for many, many years had been one called *Leaving Me Now* by a band called Level 42. It is a tide of emotion about being left by a lover while you still love them. I always adored it but was happy in the knowledge that I had never actually been left by a lover: it was always me doing the dumping, as such! Well, in the middle of my menopause my second marriage came under terrific strain and it seemed to be falling apart. I was sure it could be fixed but one morning when my radio alarm went off, my song came on the radio. At this time it was 22 years old and not played much. The lyrics 'So I suppose, you're leaving me now' belted out of the radio. Yes, you've guessed…he left that morning. Boy, was the Universe having a laugh! I was laughing and crying all at the same time! (Happy ending…he came back!)

So you see, words and lyrics can have an amazing sense of expression and to use them as a way to predict or understand something is something I am very happy to do. Bibliomancy in some ways has become more prevalent now with oracle cards and animal cards where we choose a daily card and go to the book to see what it tells us. Some of these decks are quite twee though and never give anything other than an inspirational, positive answer: All is good! God loves you: The Angel of Awareness is with you, etc. This is fine as inspiration but not really for balanced prediction.

To use bibliomancy properly there must be an element of randomness. There is no point in simply letting a book fall open at a page if you read it a lot and have a favorite passage. It will always open at that or those pages. So you need to find a way of introducing chance. This can be done by using dice or even random numbers that come into your head to show a page number and a line number to read from. You can also use a fine needle, shut your eyes and push it into the book, open it and point the needle at a line on the page. Then read on.

The week I chose to do my experiment with bibliomancy was

one where I was doing a nine-day devotion to my Goddess and also was on holiday. As well as meditations, I was meeting friends, sorting out the promotion for a new book and trying to improve my health. An ideal time to be guided.

I decided that my bibliomancy texts would be a mixture of spiritual and non-spiritual and that I would also at least once allow a random song on the radio to inspire me.

The texts I chose were to see if you really needed to stick with a spiritual book or if popular fiction could be just as relevant. So, after my daughter, an English literature student, had accrued *Fifty Shades of Grey* to see how badly it had been written, I stole it before it went into the bin. I also borrowed my other daughter's *Good News Bible* and selected my book of animal totems, *Animal Speak* by Ted Andrews. I chose one of my favorite fiction books, *Of Bees and Mist* by Erick Setiawan and added *Goddess Durga and Sacred Female Power* by Laura Amazzone. All ready and set!

On my first day I had been doing meditations and focusing on the progress of my latest book. I decided to ask if I was handling it the best way and for general advice from the Universe. I had put symbols representing each divination book on some stones and added one for 'radio.' I held them in my hands, shook them around and then let them drop. The one nearest me was chosen as the book I would use and was *Of Bees and Mist*. Then I decided on the needle approach.

Gasp! It says, 'What a flair you have for language, Meridia. Did you learn this from your mother?' I think I will take this as the Universe telling me that I am writing good books and to be confident in my words. And yes...I did learn my love of books and writing from my mother. She taught me new words every month from her *Reader's Digest* and was never without a book in her hands. I am seriously impressed. I asked about my books and got a direct answer about language. I am very happy with this divinatory experience so far!

The second day of my holiday was spent visiting a Hindu

mandir as part of a devotion to the Goddess Durga. I had been focusing on my health as I had found the walk to the temple taxing and was breathless. I have a sedentary lifestyle due to arthritis and am overweight. So I focused on health and dropped my stones and the book I was requested to use was *Goddess Durga and Sacred Female Power*. Well, I now had a one in five chance of drawing this as the previous book's stone had been removed. But I was still impressed that after my visit to the mandir to pray to Durga, her book was chosen.

The answer to my health question was, 'Power from within is not a power of control, but one which comes from valuing self, community and experience. It is the power that can heal and renew.' So, once again my question had been answered in words that referred to it, for instance, health and healing. These words spoke volumes to me. I don't value myself enough to find time to exercise in my busy life. I know I have real power when I focus it. Yet, more often than not I don't focus it for myself. Point taken, Durga! Tomorrow I will attempt my cross trainer again. I see this again as a success for the art of bibliomancy!

Day three of my bibliomancy experiment started off with me feeling very tired and slightly out of sorts. The spiritual devotions are taking it out of me emotionally, I feel tired and my irritable bowel has flared up. Yet today I have a newspaper column to write and a concert to go to, as well as a multitude of errands to run. I also feel guilty that I have not had much time with my husband lately and yet I haven't much time for the connection today. So I wanted general advice from my divinatory tool. I shook and dropped my stones and *Animal Speak* by Ted Andrews was to be my guide. The animal totem was 'raven' and the passage read, 'Raven teaches us how to take that which is unformed and give it the form you desire.'

Well, my newspaper column isn't 'formed' yet so I will ask raven to help me with that so that it can be done quickly and without distractions. I can surely manage some lunch with my lovely husband if I try hard enough and I know that my concert will lift my spirits. So this advice is good, yet not that specific. I will read more about raven today and see what else is relevant as the day goes on. Not totally impressed though I did ask for general advice and I received general advice back.

Day four dawns and I am physically tired after a brilliant Level 42 concert where dancing was not an option! I have many little tasks to do today but when I open my purse I realize that I have very little money left. Last night has blown my holiday budget. So I feel I need to ask the Universe for some guidance on finances and how to bring more abundance into my life so that happy events like seeing my favorite band can be accessible. Only three stones left and the one that falls closest to me indicated that *Fifty Shades of Grey* will be my oracle for today. If this works it will be a miracle.

The bibliomancy phrase chosen says, 'This is normality. It's so grounding after the last 48 hours of...madness.' It kind of makes sense really. In the last 48 hours I have had an expensive Brazilian meal and been to an expensive concert with drinks and travel costs. That is not normal for me as I am a frugal person. Today, needing to buy bread and milk is normal. And yes, I am feeling the need to be grounded today as although the busy time has been great fun, it has also been draining as I live rurally and the city was very busy and intense. I just hope that the oracle doesn't mean that my purse being empty will continue to be 'normal.' Once again, I feel that the Universe has responded to my question and it wasn't even with a spiritual text.

Day five and I wake up shattered and feeling every bit of my 51 years. I have walked more, danced more and socialized more in the last 4 days than in the last 6 months! I have also been meditating and doing devotions and I just feel completely worn out. Yet, I have niggling, silly worries: I have ironing to do, writing to do, dinner to cook, emails to answer, a book launch to plan and am feeling a bit overwhelmed. This is meant to be my time off...yet today, I feel tired and pressurized! So, I really need advice on this. The bibliomancy text for today is the Bible. I hope it delivers as it is one of the most popular books used in bibliomancy and I do need help with my tiredness and stress today.

The words I have chosen are, 'Don't be angry with me; don't turn your servant away.' I thought on this but it doesn't resonate with me today. The only thing I can take from it is that when I become overwhelmed, I can feel angry with myself and short-tempered with others. So maybe I need to be nicer to myself and avoid being curt with others today. I will try.

Last day of this form of divination and I hope I will have good advice. I went to bed last night worried about the amount of practical, monotonous work I have to do including tax returns. I decided to listen to the lyrics of the song on the radio when my alarm went off. I didn't sleep well though and was up and out well before my alarm call. I was driving to the supermarket from my wee village and the winter sun was shining on the fields and cows and sheep. The hills were magnificent and the air was crisp and fresh. I was humbled by the beauty around me in this wonderful Clyde Valley. When I parked at the supermarket I had the awesome feeling of all the beauty of nature but also a niggling annoyance at having to be inside and working all day. Then I remember that I hadn't had my divinatory advice for the day. So I switched on the car radio and the song playing was *Sir Duke* by Stevie Wonder. The lyrics were 'You can feel it all over; you can feel it all over, people.' It was so clear to me. This 'wonderful' feeling of the beauty and connection with nature was mine to tap into even when I had to work inside. I could use the memory to 'feel' it any time I wanted. This gift of awe at Mother Nature's prettiness could be used when I was bored or restless or caught up in tax returns. I only need to stop and access it! So, a simple lyric has fired me up for the day and given me a way to tackle the mundane and the boring tasks we all have to do in life. Thank you, Universe! Thank you, Stevie!

After six days of bibliomancy revelations I am now converted. This has been a real eye opener for me and I have enjoyed it so much. I feel I will expand on it too. Maybe a line at random from my newspaper? A more intense look at what MTV or radio has to say to me? I won't overuse it but I can see that when chance presents a phrase or lyric that I will think more deeply on what is being said to me.

Chapter 7

Dowsing

Pendulous Pendulums and Twitchy Twigs

Dowsing or divining is the practice of finding things by paranormal means usually using a pendulum or dowsing rods. These again are only tools though and dowsing should be able to be done without them. People have been known to be able to find water underground and animals seem to have a natural skill for this. Obviously some people are better than others at dowsing and may have a natural ability to find water, ancient sacred sites and archaeological remains. There have been men who have made their fortune by being able to sense where oil is present underground. This is called doodle bugging. But we all can't be J.R. Ewing from Dallas!

Dowsing can give us the answer to where things are, find lost objects and even help in healing. I would think that most natural healers would be natural dowsers too. In fact some healers use crystal pendulums as part of their diagnostic tool kit. The client would lie flat and the healer would pass a pendulum over their body to see where any blockages or odd energies were located. This would be sensed by the movement of the pendulum or a 'pull' down towards the area of disease. Some healers use a crystal wand or simply use their hands.

The art of dowsing can also pick up on paranormal activity and help locate ley lines. Ley lines are natural paths of earth energy and can not only affect the feel of a place but can also affect people living on or near them. Spirits can be more active near ley lines and the buildup of energy can attract poltergeist activity. It can also lead to headaches, weird energy draining illnesses and tension. So it can be good to know if you live or work on a ley line and more so if it is where ley lines cross where there is double whammy of power. I am not sure that much can be done, although amethyst crystals can absorb some of the energy and smudging with white sage can help too. I know of someone who buries copper pipes around properties on ley lines in an attempt to bend the ley line around them. I am not sure how successful this actually can be as in my experience ley lines are massive energies and I don't feel a few metal rods could realign them.

Pendulum divination is probably one of the most accessible and immediate ways of allowing our subconscious to communicate with us. We have answers within our subconscious that can be accessed by asking our pendulum to answer for us. Pendulums can also be used to seek answers from higher energies or universal forces and can be very accurate as long as the right questions have been asked in the first place. They can also be used to find a lost object, help choose between life options and in healing therapies.

A pendulum can be bought in many New Age shops and on the Internet and some are very pretty and ornate. Yet all you really need for a pendulum is a weighted, symmetric object (the bob) and a chain of some sort. The bob has to weigh enough for it to pull down and stay stationary but also has to be light enough to respond to minute changes in energy. Brass has been traditionally used but most pendulums today are made from crystal drops either wrapped in a metal cage or with a clasp attached to them.

My first pendulum was simply my wedding ring looped through a chain and dangled above my pregnant tummy to see if I was carrying a girl or a boy. I hadn't charged it up or asked it for its directions for boy or girl. I was relying on the traditional interpretation of circular movement for a girl and back/forth for a boy. Needless to say it gave me confusing and mysterious answers.

A pendulum needs to be charged or tuned into its user's

energy, and correct answers only come from conversation and some set rules, which are agreed on between the pendulum and its owner. Therefore, pendulums are not transferable between people and I have never allowed anyone to handle mine.

Buy your pendulum or make one and then sit at a flat table or surface and really feel the energy between yourself and your pendulum. Hold your pendulum between your thumb and forefinger on your writing hand. Leave about six to ten inches of chain available between you and the bob. You can tune a pendulum in by either asking it to show you its 'yes/no' responses or by telling it what you would want to see for the same. I have always found that it is better to let my pendulum tell me what it wants. When asked for a 'yes' answer my pendulum started to swing in clockwise circles. A weak movement indicated a weak 'yes' and a big massive swirly circle indicated a very definite 'yes.' For a 'no' response my pendulum moved back and forth in a horizontal direction. If it did a bit of something in the middle, for example, a mild circle with some back/forwards sweeps, then I took it that there wasn't meant to be an answer at that time or that I hadn't asked a defined enough question.

Once your pendulum has told you what it wants then you can start to use it for 'yes/no' questions for yourself. If you choose to tell it what you want from its movements then make sure you confirm it is responding by asking it some questions that you already know the answer to and checking it is being honest! Practice makes perfect and it is important to really build up a relationship with your pendulum. We can influence a pendulum's movement with our own subconscious fears or desires so make sure you are in a completely honest and relaxed frame of mind when you ask for advice.

You can use the simple 'yes/no' question to begin with but make sure the question is not open ended. 'Will I move house?' may well bring a 'yes' answer (yes at some point you will move house), but if your question is really, 'Will I move house in the next six months?' then you may have a 'no' answer. Always put timing into your question if you can or you could have a misleading result simply due to not being specific enough. Do not ask negative questions, for example, 'Will I not move house?' as the answers can be confusing just because of the terminology.

Pendulums can be used far more creatively though and have helped me many times in my clairvoyant practice in the past although I must admit I haven't used one for a while as my tarot cards have proved so accurate. You can divine a correct choice using a pendulum by allowing it to swing over options written on pieces of paper. If, for instance, you have three houses you could move to, then ask the pendulum a straightforward question, such as, 'What house would make the best long-term home for me?' Let the pendulum hover over all choices and watch for the best and clearest 'yes' answer. It is best to lay the choices face down and hidden from you after having mixed them up. That way your own conscious mind won't influence the answer. The same can be done with jobs, holiday locations and even romantic potentials! Remember to respect your pendulum as it is a conduit of your inner consciousness. Asking about whether you should have a burger or a pizza meal is simply not on!

I have had amazing results by separating out four tarot cards that show particular options and turning them over and shuffling them. I placed them face down with no idea which one was in what position and asked a pertinent question. I then suspended the pendulum over each card until I saw the best or only 'yes' answer. Then I turned the card over and interpreted its meaning. In this way you are combining two forms of divination, which can give very clear answers if only you have the confidence to do so.

I have used my pendulum with an ordinance survey map to pin down potential flood areas, toxicity and sacred sites. I have also used it to point out potentially negative neighbors in an area and also to give information to an adopted child as to where to start looking for her birth parent. Looking back at these experiences I am sad that I gradually lost the connection with my pendulum. It needs to come out more and be used as an integral part of readings.

Dowsing Rods

A dowsing rod can be simply a Y shaped twig from a living tree. Hazel and willow are the most commonly used. The top of the Y is held in either hand and the dowser walks around the area where he suspects he may find water underground. The tip of the Y shape will bend down or twitch when the element is located. Alternatively dowsing rods can be two L shaped rods of metal where the short part of the L is held in the hands and the long part is able to swing free. With L shaped rods the movement can be far more extreme than with Y shaped. The nearer you are to what you are searching, the more the rods will cross over one another. If you are further away, the rods can both move in harmony towards the left or right and have been known to even turn backwards to point out that you have gone too far!

If you think I am overenthusiastic about dowsing rods, it is because I have used them and seen others work with them and have been amazed. My first premises as a clairvoyant were in an old building that had so many areas of spiritual activity that it was joyfully active. I ran psychic development classes and one evening I decided to show my students how to dowse. I already knew where the 'hot' spots of activity were and hoped that dowsing would show these up.

The students were asked to bring an old wire coat hanger. This was then cut with wire cutters and bent into two L shaped rods. I didn't want the students to be able to influence them too much by holding them either too tight to prevent movement or to let their own fears or excitement force movement. To prevent this I provided plastic drinking straws for the short part of the L shape to sit in and these were held by the student. This meant that when the rods were held level that any movement was not influenced by the person. And, oh my, did this work!

As my small band of students went off in different directions in the old building, there were many screams and much laughter too as the rods started to rotate and pull them in the direction of the spirit energies. Exactly at the points I knew there was activity, the rods crossed and stayed that way. I asked students to walk backwards and the rods uncrossed. Moving forwards, they crossed again! Most were stunned and repeated the dowsing experiment just to achieve the same results. Dowsing was one form of divination in the development class where most, if not all students, could see a response. Why not try it?

I had decided to put my pendulum to use for a client who needed some answers to some questions. Normally I would have my full tarot deck to help with this so I felt a bit 'naked' with only my new pendulum, which had chosen me at a spiritual health fayre the previous week. So I decided to use a mix of tarot and pendulum divination. I chose four random cards from the tarot deck and placed them face down on the table. I didn't see what they were. Then I focused on the client and her question and let the pendulum hang over each card until some movement was detected. This is what happened.

Kate had four main questions which needed to be honed down and made as direct as possible.

The first one was, 'Will there be real happiness in my future?'

The pendulum hardly moved over three of the cards at all but when placed above one of them it started to move. However, it started to spin anticlockwise which threw me off a bit as it is normally clockwise for a yes answer. So I thought that maybe this was going to be a negative in whatever the card suggested. The card was the 'worry' card so I felt the answer was simply,

'Don't worry.' Kate needs to stop worrying and accept that life will bring her the happiness she so deserves.

Kate's second question was, 'Do you see me with a nice partner in the future?'

Again, there was no movement for three out of the four face-down tarot cards but the pendulum spun very decidedly clockwise at one of them. It was the Knight of Discs card that can represent a very earthy and genuine male over about 40 who is caring, practical and dependable. He may also be an earth sign: Taurus, Capricorn or Virgo. So that is a YES then.

Kate was going away on a special weekend linked to a hobby and wondered if it would be memorable for more than the hobby?

Again the pendulum swung anticlockwise and I took this as a warning about the card. When I turned the card it was the Knight of Swords which represents a male who can be intellectual or wise about his known subjects and also can be quite charismatic and witty. They can also be air signs: Aquarius, Gemini or Libra. So Kate would need to be wary of being maybe taken in by this sort of male. In being given the heads up she can now go and enjoy her weekend without being distracted by someone who would not make it memorable.

The last question was a big one and I was not sure that the pendulum could really answer. It was, 'What is my life's purpose?' At one card the pendulum started moving back and forth which is my 'NO' answer. So I thought maybe no answer would be given but when I turned the card I chose to interpret this differently. The card was 'The Wheel of Fortune' and I chose to interpret this as saying that Kate's life purpose was not fated but rather was within her own control. Kate's circumstances dictate who she needs to be for now but I believe that this answer is saying that she is not defined by that and can make life whatever she wants.

The pendulum/card combination gave some interesting answers, but felt too vague for me. Let's see what Kate thinks?

After sending the questions I was curious as I have never had a reading done with a pendulum. Colette, it was amazing!!!! The answers were so true i.e., I am always worrying about something and I know I have to do less.

The reading was straight to the point and I could connect with what you were telling me. I found the pendulum and tarot cards together a very, very interesting reading.

Was exciting to read especially when the pendulum was swinging anticlockwise had a wee shiver!!! Ohh what's it going to say!!! I am more than happy with my reading, I'm content to go away on my weekend now. And to do some soul searching with my life. Once again, Colette, thank you. x

Chapter 8

Shaman Bones

Finding Your Inner Witch Doctor

Shaman bones are sometimes called witch doctor bones but this term is too small as many cultural shamans use bones for divination, not just witch doctors that are more traditionally associated with African magic. Dried bones can look stunning and have been used for the decoration of shamans as long as there have been shamans, which is a very long time!

Bones are said to contain great power and also to connect us to the animal's spirit. The Hoodoo term for this is 'ashe' which in simple terms means power. The bones of an animal can be used to connect to one's animal totem or spirit ally, but they can also be used for divination and/or magic. Obviously there are all sorts of ethics that need to be considered and what may have been acceptable in the past is not in many cases acceptable now. Crushed rhinoceros horn, elephant tusk or tiger bones seem downright squalid now. In the past items made from bones of rare animals were traded and sold for large amounts of money. People believed in the power in them. This is now illegal, but the trade still thrives in some countries.

Yet today, it is highly unlikely in Western society to come across a shaman bone reader. This is due to it falling out of favor due to societal changes and ecological viewpoints. Yet in many cultures this type of reading is the main one and seems to produce excellent results.

I had a Nigerian client who heard that my husband, a shaman, worked with shaman bones and immediately asked for this rather than my tarot reading. I had a witch doctor bone reading done by a clairvoyant many years ago and was very impressed but again, this woman was a good clairvoyant and I feel she could have turned her hand to many divinatory tools.

It was time to make my own shaman bones and I wasn't looking forward to it. I would never harm an animal for any divinatory purpose so I decided to make my bones from our Sunday roast chicken's carcass. First I boiled the bones to remove the last meat from them and then set the ones I was going to use aside to dry thoroughly on a warm windowsill. This didn't go down well with my daughter who was appalled and threatened never to bring her friends home again. After a week the bones were very clean, dry and a bit bleached by the sunlight. I followed instructions from my husband who had made his own shaman bones set many years ago.

Basically, we are making a 'family' of bones so you need two ancestor/grandparent bones, two parent bones and two children bones. The grandparent bones are made from broken breast bones. The parent bones are made from the two hip bones and the children bones are made from two thigh bones. All bones are marked as either male or female. This is decided by intuition and the way the bone feels, is shaped or by differences in tone or color. Each bone is marked at the top too to show which way is up. I did this with red nail polish which was close at hand after my manicure.

There also needs to be at least three other random bones chosen, which represent luck, love and health. You can do more if you want but this was already looking quite complicated! Each of these bones was marked with a symbol that represented these qualities.

You need something to wrap them in, which can also be used as some sort of template for the reading. I chose a lovely embroidered napkin. My template was made by using my medicine wheel and the associated four directions: spirituality, emotions, physical and intellect. The reading I had received in the past also included some crystals so I added some of my favorites: sodalite for truth; iron pyrites or fool's gold for lies; citrine for energy/confidence; Apache Tear for sorrow and amethyst for spirituality. I felt with the bones and the crystals I would have enough randomness to see patterns and therefore divine readings more accurately. It is thought that shaman bones that were marked on different sides with color or symbols were the beginning of divination with dice.

The readings themselves are done differently by different shamans. The way shown to me involved the following.

The grandparent bones can represent the past or the root of the question.

The parent bones can represent the present and also the way forward with the issues. The child bones can represent the future or the outcome of the question.

The other three bones will represent the energy of the outcome e.g. fortunate, healthy and loving or the opposite if reversed. Also, there can be general divination done by seeing where the bones fall on the template and also how they interact with one another and the crystals. The key is about patterns and the interrelationship of the bones. Use the parent bone to represent the client by choosing male or female and watch what other bones fall around it. In this way you can build up knowledge of certain patterns that mean, for example, a woman has children or a husband/partner and what issues there may be depending on what part of the template the bones fall in.

If a question is asked about money, for instance, you could see where the luck bone lies, and if a question is about health you could see where the client's bone landed on the template, which may perhaps be in the physical direction or in the mental direction. If a question is about deception in a relationship then see what crystal lies next to the two parent bones e.g. sodalite for truth or fool's gold for deceit.

I began to feel quite excited about this form of divination as it seemed to me to have enough potential for really accurate answers.

Initially I had agreed to read for Adam but his wife came along and had an associated question so I decide to read for them both.

Adam's question was a simple one. He wanted to know if the house that they had viewed and wanted to move into was going to happen although various things seemed to be hindering the completion of tenancy.

Adam held all the bones and crystals in his hands and focused on the question. He shook them and then let them fall onto the template cloth. The first bone that caught my eye was the love bone laying very definitely in the west of my template, which is the area of the physical and property. This showed that Adam had really connected with the house and that it would be a good move for him if possible.

Two of the female bones (the parent and child) were touching but upside down. This meant that his intuition on the house move and his doubts of it completing were probably correct. To confirm this, both these bones were touching the Apache Tear crystal which is the representation of sorrow. So to be honest, it looked as though the particular house would be lovely for him but just wasn't going to be his.

The male parent bone was facing south and touching the sodalite crystal, which is the truth crystal. I interpreted this to mean that he should look in an area south of the house he would miss out on and would find something just as good.

Adam's reply

Good Grief! I am the type of person that likes a straight answer and not fluff. Brilliant; that's exactly what I needed and wanted and got. I could see eventually where Colette was getting things from but getting that information like that from a small pile of bones – wonderful. Pretty entertaining too!

Adam's wife is Elaine and her question was again about a house move but more about how it would enable her to achieve her desires. Elaine is self-employed and was hoping that by moving house that she could set up new work patterns as she had a few health concerns and wasn't coping well with her working week, which could stretch to 24/7 and was leaving her depressed.

Again she focused on her question and shook the bones and then let them fall on the template.

Although there was a middle cluster, two main aspects were sitting very far out on the template. The luck bone was reversed in the north indicating that a move north at this time would not be auspicious. Her own bone, the female parent, was sitting in the south showing a clear path for her. I asked her if she fantasized about moving to the north of Scotland and she said yes. This might be an option in the future but not now. She is meant to be staying south, which was good as it matched up with Adam's direction!

In the center, there was an intense combination of the fool's gold crystal with the male ancestor bone. I wondered if she maybe was deceiving herself about wanting to slow down in work and if she actually was a workaholic! This attitude could have come from her father and I asked her to look into her father's relationship to work. She smiled and looked away at this comment.

Right in the middle of the template was the citrine crystal showing that Elaine has confidence, enthusiasm and drive for anything she believes in and her core value is one of giving 110 percent. This was worrying as the health bone was reversed next to it showing that this attitude was, in fact, now detrimental to her health. It could also be read that her health could indeed be a barrier to career success if she didn't work on changing her core value a bit and also working on her family work traditions or attitudes.

There was also a painful combination of the Apache Tear crystal for sadness sitting beside the sodalite or truth crystal. This told me that in accepting the truth of her situation, there would be tears and unhappiness. Elaine likes her work and thrives in the creativity and enthusiasm of her business. But her health is now not up to old work patterns and she will need to let go of some of her deep held desires for excellence. She needs to put health first now. Elaine also needs to look at the way she defines herself by success at work and her standing in her work community. I think there may be perfectionism there that is truly wearing her out.

The female ancestor bone was in the west, the area of health in my template. I felt this meant that she should take a leaf out of her mother's book where attitudes are concerned and not her dad's. She should also be aware of hereditary illness through her mum's side.

In answer to her question about the house move, the shaman bones were a bit more intense than just a straight yes or no. They were telling Elaine that she had to make this house move the start of new work patterns that would allow her to have decent health. There really was no option but it would be down to her to make it work and be disciplined in finding a balance.

Elaine's reply

My goodness. I am stunned by how much information this short reading actually delivered. It was a bit blunt but I can relate to all of it. I have always wanted to move to the north of Scotland but my work needs me to be in the central belt for now. I do realize that my health isn't very good and has the potential to become worse. This frightens me and I sometimes choose just to ignore it and keep going. This has led to collapse at times. My dad worked constantly and would have gone into work with his leg hanging off if he had to. My mum was more relaxed and would take time out for herself. My hereditary problems do actually come from my mum's side and they will only get worse. I loved the way the bones picked up on the differing attitudes between my dad and mum.

I do define myself a lot by my performance at work. I know this is wrong. And I am a perfectionist. I know it will be hard for me to get off the bandwagon and accept a gentler way of life, but I do want it now. And I know my health needs it. I will do my best to let go and be disciplined in cutting back.

Thanks Colette xx

Chapter 9

Too Taboo to Do!

Many forms of divination from the past would simply be considered too taboo to be undertaken now. The use of a dead body just wouldn't be all right at all. The sacrificing of an animal and then the reading of its entrails goes against our love of animals and indeed this practice has been outlawed in most parts of the world now. It would also be quite hard to have clients who wanted spatulamancy, which involved using skin, bone or poo! Not really the type of person I would want to read for!

Necromancy

The art of divination where the dead are conjured up or magically called is not the same, in my opinion, as mediumship. Necromancy is when there is the clear intent to bring the dead forth from where they reside and gain information from them either about a situation or the future. There is a sense of abuse of power in this. How would you feel if you were happily or unhappily doing your spiritual business and someone whisked you from it and demanded to know things that you knew and they desired. It doesn't seem very polite to me. Yet as a medium I do communicate with spirits on many levels of their journeys.

Mediumship is when there is a sense of connection with spirits and is practiced in spiritualist churches in many countries and in many clairvoyant and mediumship practices. I have never known a spirit who wasn't an evolved higher being like a spirit guide giving information on the future. They just seem to give messages that they are all right and not to worry. Some give proof of who they are and some tell stories from the past or present to show that they are still a part of the bereaved person's life. So I believe that the dead on the first few levels of their journey have some sort of ethical code that prevents them influencing the future by what they could say. This doesn't mean that they can't be around and guide through empathy or look after us and help us out of harm's way. Higher evolved beings, such as spirit guides, seem to be able to communicate potential future events so maybe this is an 'earned' or learned ability with time in the spiritual plane.

In all the time I have been a clairvoyant working mediumistically I have never called a spirit towards me in any way. I have opened my mind and my heart and asked for a connection, if that be their will, never using their name. That to me is the difference between something honest and right and something that is an abuse of power. Drawing the dead from their healing or work could be catastrophic. I have a very personal story with which to illustrate this.

Many years ago when my younger daughter was about four years old and I was working as a clairvoyant, something happened to make me very against anyone who would call a spirit towards them using their name. There was a little girl in our family who had died tragically and had become quite a pleasant spirit to have around. On my trip to my consulting office, she would often appear in my car and then help out with the readings that night. She seemed to enjoy being part of it all. One evening, on my way to work, she appeared in my car and shouted my younger daughter's name out loud and then disappeared. Well, I felt ill and stopped the car to phone home where my husband was looking after my daughter. The phone rang out again and again and I decided to turn the car round and go straight home. Something bad must have happened for the spirit to shout and disappear like that. Eventually my husband answered the phone and said everything was all right but he was shocked. My daughter had been playing on her trike in our quiet cul de sac and had shot off the pavement into the path of a lone taxi. Instead of landing under the wheel, her bike kind of twisted and was sent flying back onto the pavement. She was shocked and had some scratches but all the neighbors who had seen the accident couldn't understand why she wasn't dead. I knew exactly why. My little spirit helper had gone to her assistance.

If the same scenario had happened but say the spirit's mum had been to someone who was calling her or conjuring her up, would my daughter's plight have been different? I feel strongly it may have been. My daughter had a family spirit looking out for her and that spirit was free to be where she wanted to be at that time. So therefore, never call or pull a spirit towards you. You don't know what other jobs they may have at hand at that time!

Anthropomancy

It is hard to believe that humans would sacrifice other humans for the sake of divination. Wouldn't it just have been easier to look at the stars or look into a pool of water? Yet in some ancient civilizations, the seer would command attention of the ruler by human sacrifice and then divine from the entrails. This was called anthropomancy. It was believed that young, virginal children made the best bodies for this hideous art. The liver was seen as the place where the soul resided and as such was the major organ used. It was cut up and aligned with planetary positions and the auspices were read by no doubt very egocentric priests.

As haruspicy or extispicy, this technique was performed on animal sacrifices too. Goats and sheep had quite large livers and so were the animals of preference. Bird entrails were used too. We cannot conceive of these taboo divinatory practices in this modern age. Some of these practices were more about the sense of power of the priests who performed them. They caused people to be frightened and be in awe of the person who could perform them. This enhanced the probability that the prediction would be believed. No doubt there was more of a theatrical element in extispicy than say, ovomacy, or divining with an egg! Most of the above practices have been outlawed in progressive societies but some animal sacrifices have only recently been banned in religious festivals in parts of Asia. Occasionally we hear of a terrible story where it is indicated that a child murder has been linked to a religious sacrifice and augury. No human or animal should be hurt for divinatory purposes. It is obscene and linked to the past when we didn't know better. Or maybe we did, but the human ego simply didn't care.

Scatomancy

Divination by Poo, anyone? No...I didn't think so! The divinatory art of scatomancy is the reading of excrement for the purpose of prediction or health insights. Now in some ways this is still done by medical professionals as scatology, where the feces are examined for signs of blood, protein and mucus which can be indicative of poor bowel health. I have just had a kit delivered by the NHS as I am now over fifty and am to be screened for bowel cancer. This I can accept although I haven't yet been able to bring myself to go to work with the little plate and scraper! But using poo for divination seems simply a step too far!

The Ancient Egyptians let their dung beetles loose on excrement and watched not only their movements but also the shapes that were left behind after their work. These dung beetles were seen as sacred and can be seen in hieroglyphics and read about in Egyptian texts. Yet, I could find very few references to the actual symbols involved.

A doctor may look for evidence of blood or illness but what could be used for prediction of events? The shape of the poo? Its smell? Its texture? Or the sound of the motion hitting the toilet pan? Definitely one to miss, I think. My stomach wouldn't take it and I really don't feel that there would be client demand. Thank goodness!

Chapter 10

Omens and Superstitions

An omen is believed to be a sign that can foretell the future. Omens can be good or bad and can mean very different things depending on culture or country. A superstition is the belief that one event/experience can lead to another in the future. With superstitions there is 'cause and effect,' for instance, if you do 'this'...then the outcome will be 'that.' Normally superstitions are about preventing bad luck. I think in our modern day, omens are seen as more weighty and dramatic and superstitions seen as a bit lowbrow and farcical, arising from fear or ignorance.

A certain unusual astrological pattern like a grand cross could be seen as an omen and the belief that black cats are bad /good luck could be seen as a superstition.

Throughout history omens have been reported to have been linked to important events. Certain battles or world events have been presaged by astrological events, such as solar eclipses or comets. Kings would be crowned on auspicious days decided by their court astrologers and magicians; marriages would be blessed or cursed by the weather or unusual happenings. A comet was meant to presage the death of a king or nobleman. Possibly the most debated omen of our times has been the end of the Mayan calendar and the belief that the world would somehow end on the 21st of December 2012.

Superstitions are of more interest to me. I live in a house where my daughter salutes single magpies and asks you to break her finger circle to break the bad luck. I become excited if my left hand itches because I believe money is coming my way and very disappointed if it is my right hand as money will flow away from me. Likewise, if my ears burn, then someone is talking about me. A black cat is lucky if it crosses my path and I almost stalk my neighbor's cat on her morning walk. Yet most people avoid black cats as they believe they are bad luck. This could be linked to the belief that they are witches' familiars or shape shifting witches.

If I spill salt then it is thrown over my left shoulder to reverse the bad luck. I avoid breaking mirrors and never walk under a ladder. Shoes are not allowed on tables and no umbrella will ever be open inside my house! Spiders will never be killed and soup is always stirred clockwise. We take great pleasure on wishing on the wishbone of the Sunday roast chicken. This is very tongue in cheek yet some households do take their superstitions very seriously.

Most of these superstitions have been passed down through my family and been absorbed through day-to-day living with older parents. But now I hear myself saying the same things to my own children and know they, in turn, will pass them on too. There is a kind of comfort with superstitions that can give a very tenable link to our pasts, our families and our culture.

At Hogmanay, New Year's Eve in Scotland, I still open the back door to let the old year out and then open the front door to let the New Year in. Pans and pots are bashed and rattled to help the old year on its way. It is preferable if the first visitor after midnight the 'First Foot' is a tall dark man carrying a lump of coal and a tot of whisky for wealth and luck. Of course, the house will have been cleaned thoroughly beforehand so that I can maintain a clean tidy home for the whole year ahead. This, I have to say, has never been a superstition that actually worked for me.

So where do superstitions come from? Some may just be ways of educating us to avoid risky things. Walking under a ladder may be unlucky for the person standing on it if you happen to startle them. A paint pot could be dropped on your head as a result and a trip to Accident and Emergency ensue. Yet it is also thought that a ladder against a wall is the shape of a triangle, which represents the Holy Trinity and it would be blasphemous to walk through it. There is also a link to the shape of the hangman's gallows.

Some people won't get out of bed on Friday the 13th. We all blame any bad luck that happens on that day simply on the day itself. But this luck surely would have happened anyway. Or would it? I believe chaos brings further chaos and if you go out on Friday the 13th full of anxiety and nervous energy, then you will attract that sort of chaos and maybe actually have more bad luck than normal. So I make an effort to avoid even thinking about the date in unlucky terms and normally breeze through it. Again there is a link to Christianity, this time regarding the Last Supper and the thirteen people at the table, one of whom Jesus was about to be crucified. Most dinner party hosts avoid thirteen guests and some restaurants don't have a table '13.'

Mirrors are believed to reflect the soul so when one is broken it means that the soul is broken too. This can bring very bad luck; normally seven years of it! Some people cover mirrors when a person dies at home so that their soul will not become trapped. The soul can be released from the mirror by scraping it against wood especially that of a tree in a cemetery. The spirit of the wood can work magic on the soul to release it. Another thought is that Jesus died on the cross and the cross was made of wood and therefore wood holds the key to the resurrection of the spirit or soul.

Amulets are objects which are seen to give protection to people who believe in them. An amulet is normally a naturally occurring object or one made to represent a belief system. Talismans are similar but are empowered by someone who knows how to energize them, such as a shaman or magician. Some relics of saints are seen to empower the wearer and allow their prayers to be heard by the particular saint.

Amulets tend to be worn on the person whereas talismans can be worn or placed near the person or in homes. So-called lucky charms can be amulets or talismans. Some people wear a lucky rabbit's foot, some maybe a cross, Eye of Horus, pentagram, scarab beetle or tree of life. Some sportsmen may wear lucky underpants, the same color vest or have a lucky golf club. Empowered talismans are more likely to have stronger power due to the person knowing that they have been charged up for the purpose. Lucky charms do seem to bring luck but some say this is due to the psychological effect of feeling you have some control over the chaotic world.

I can truly feel the differences in power between my small picture of Durga that I carry in my purse and the Durga Yantra on my altar that has been empowered by a Hindu priest. There is yet another level of power in my prayer beads that were blessed for me at the River Ganges during Navratri festival. Blessed items can make people feel safe and protected. Although Catholicism frowns on talismans and says that any protection is because of faith, not the empowered talisman itself, I know many Catholics who hold their crucifixes and rosary beads during times of chaos and this, I believe, does empower these objects. In fact, many religious talismans are so empowered by the person's own belief that they radiate immense energy. This is as true for a Christian with a cross, a pagan with a pentagram, an Egyptian with an Ankh or a tribal shaman with tattoos of his gods/goddesses of nature on his body. To believe something is lucky or protective empowers it and this can empower the person to have confidence and inner power.

Lucky charms aren't a bad thing unless the 'empowerer' is trying to get money out of you and threatens bad luck if you don't buy. I remember once being approached by a traveler in quite a threatening way, near my clairvoyant premises and being asked to buy a small plastic charm for £5 because 'I needed the luck.' I replied that I already had a lucky charm and didn't need another one. The woman asked me who had made it for me to which I replied, 'Colette the clairvoyant' as I had made myself a runic talisman earlier that week. The woman said, 'Oh Colette. I know her well. She taught me how to make charms so you will be safe buying from me.' I couldn't believe her cheek and walked away laughing as she shouted out that I was now cursed for not buying from her. I had never set eyes on her in my life yet she was saying that I had taught her.

Never buy something that is very expensive and never be bullied into handing money over for something which is tosh. Give your money to charity and learn how to make and empower your own talisman! The Internet is awash with so called mystics offering worthless crystals/haunted jewelry at huge prices with the promise of winning the lottery or better health. It makes me sick. Steer very clear.

Chapter 11

A Day in the Life of a Daft Diviner

So, you have a better understanding of divination now and can use augury to help you understand each day, if you choose. The problem with divination is that it can be addictive. Those who have progressed from a yearly tarot reading to a monthly, then weekly, then daily one will bear this out! So don't be tempted to become too engrossed in odd forms of divination or your day ahead could look like this:

You have to get up before the sun is up so that you can see what the cock has to crow about. You sit out in the cold and start chanting through the alphabet and where the cock crows you write the letter down (alectryomancy). This leaves you confused as you read 'BDHPRXZ' and try to make something out of it. You give up, knowing that you will have more messages as the day goes on.

First on the agenda is to see what noises your urine makes as it bubbles into your receptacle (uromancy), or maybe even how your poo looks if you can bear to look at it (scatomancy)! Both seem happy enough so you decide you may just go to that party you have been invited to later. Then you look at your face as you wash it and see a new spot on your face (maculomancy), and maybe reconsider. Yet, your teeth seem to be happy and shiny this morning (odontomancy), so maybe you will go after all.

On the way to the kitchen you listen to the growls your hungry tummy is making and try to see if you can make anything out from them (gastromancy). The sounds seem more upbeat than angry so it must portend a good day ahead. This is confirmed by the way your egg mixes in with the milk for your omelette (ovomancy), and the lovely happy circle left by your coffee dregs (cafeomancy). So far so good! Maybe you should just see how a banana peel can tell you about the party when mixed with an orange peel (fructomancy). Yep, still looking good! Now for a wee bit of bibliomancy as you open your daily newspaper and see what advice can be gleaned (bibliomancy). On page 11, eleven rows down, you look for word number 11 (numerology). The word is 'halitosis' so you go back upstairs and brush your teeth again.

You turn on your computer to check your social networking site but it won't load. Then your updates crash your PC and you are left staring at a blank screen. Is this a sign to stay in (technomancy)? Will you not be good company? Will your mind go blank when you meet someone new? Then miraculously, the social networking site comes back on bringing with it a friend's request from someone going to the party! Beauty...you must go now!

But you must be full of beans so maybe a wee sleep first. Who knows, you may dream of a new partner (oneiromamcy), or maybe the way you sleep will tell you how to approach him/ her (meconomancy).

You nearly don't go to the party due to heavy rain putting you off (hydatomancy), but are glad you do when you spot someone lovely across the room. You check them out by gazing in their eyes for clues (iridology), and checking out their lips to divine their true character (labiomancy). All looks good until you look down and see their unmatched socks and scary shoes and decide to go for someone less fashionable (stolisomancy).

In fact, you decide just to wander and enjoy the ambiance and listen for any choice phrases that people around you are whispering to one another (transataumancy). But this leads you to hear something not so very nice about yourself but you know this is just the ravings of lunatics (chresomancy)!

The party is becoming just a bit mad anyway and you think it might be time to escape. You look for clues and find it by interpreting the blood that is flowing from someone who has just been punched in the nose (dririmancy), and also the wild guffawing of drunken ex-friends (geloscopy) as they spin around to 80s music and fall down at your feet (gyromanacy). Time to leave! Too much animal like behavior going on here (zoomancy).

See what I mean?

Chapter 12

Now it is Your Turn!

Meditating Before a Reading

All divination techniques depend on the ability of the reader to tune into the messages offered. Most people would be able to learn to play the piano to a reasonable standard if they had determination but little talent. There will be many mediocre piano players for every Mozart. The same is true, I believe, for psychic ability. We all have it to some degree; some more than others. Some people will investigate it and learn certain techniques but they will never manage to be exceptional unless they have a talent for it. This is fine. It would be a boring world if we all excelled at the same thing.

Whether you want to explore the ability you have or maximize a talent, meditation is the key to reaching your goal. Although some insights will certainly come in natural environments, in dreams and at odd times, it is important to be relaxed and in the 'zone' to be able to be your best in divination. Meditation can make this happen. It helps you control intruding thoughts, center yourself and ignore outside distractions. I meditate for at least an hour before readings and also incorporate prayers of thank you and to welcome my guides. This sets the scene as such for the visions to flow and for my third eye to be open. Many people seem quite alarmed by meditation saying they can't shut off thoughts enough to meditate properly. Meditation, like everything worthwhile, takes time and patience. Below is a very easy and general meditation to try before you decide to involve yourself in any form of divination. Try it; it works!

Sacred Space Meditation

Find yourself somewhere comfortable to sit or lay down. Surround yourself with warmth and comfort, maybe some pillows and a comfy blanket. Close your eyes and say a wee prayer that the meditation will calm you and also give you any insights that you may need for the work ahead.

Now think of a place that you associate with feelings of extreme calm and serenity. It could be a place from your last holiday or simply a place that you have felt secure. It is better if it is outside in nature and not a crowded place. My sacred space is a loch that I used to visit in the Highlands of Scotland with my family and sometimes on my own. It is tranquil, very beautiful and holds so many happy memories for me. You will have some place like this that resonates with you and will be your sacred space. Now you have to travel there in your mind. Mentally close the door on your house and either go in your car or walk to it or fly away in an airplane. Make the journey pleasant as you feel the weight of worry fall away as you become excited about visiting your special place. As you arrive at your destination, stand and look at what you see. Your memory should serve you well and you will remember a special tree or the way the water looks or how the grass blows in the wind. Take in the view and breathe out and in deeply as you enjoy the vista. Now, in your head, go and sit where you would have the best outlook and can see but not be seen. This is your sacred space. No one can come into it unless you invite them. You can view things but will not be interrupted unless you want to be interrupted.

Let your gaze take you around your sacred space and see and feel what is there. What season is it? Is the wind high or low? Is the sun shining? Can you feel the earth below you and the sky above you? What do you feel? Are you sad or happy or stressed and worn out? If you have negative energy, ask the earth to take it from you. Feel it draining out of your body into the good mother earth. Or walk in the water and let the water soothe your ills. Let any negativity flow out of you.

At this point you may be drawn back into memories of why this place feels good for you. I sometimes 'see' my dad and my little spaniel walking along the loch shore and it cheers me up as this reminds me of happy times when they both walked this earth with me. Sometimes something will catch your vision; a bird may fly across your gaze or a fish may jump in the water. Enjoy whatever shows itself to you. And yet again, release what you need to release. Or simply enjoy the view. While your mind focuses on the view, you will be subconsciously relaxing and meditating without too much effort on your part.

After 15 minutes or so, or as long as it takes, start your journey back to your starting point. Stand up, say some thanks, wave goodbye to anyone you encountered and then get back in the car/plane etc and make your way home, building up energy for the day ahead. When you feel yourself back in your bed or chair, let your conscious mind take over and bring you back to reality. Open your eyes and move your muscles and stretch. Have a drink of water.

If you don't have an active imagination, you may have to practice more than someone who is good with visualization. Persevere! It will be worth it and the more you do it, it will become habit and your sacred space will be accessible to you more quickly and more dramatically. I can conjure up my sacred space within a second now if I need an instant 'calm fix.'

You don't need any crystals specifically for this meditation but I find that amethyst can be good for bringing a calm feeling and also tiger's eye can help you 'view' your sacred space in a more vibrant and real way. If you are worried that you may stay in the meditation, then hold a grounding crystal like obsidian in your hand. Make it a ragged one or one which isn't tumbled and let it make its presence felt to bring you back to your conscious mind. I quite like an obsidian arrow head…it can certainly make its presence felt by gently digging itself into your palm.

After this most basic of meditations, you should feel relaxed and maybe a bit 'out there.' Now open your third eye by closing your eyes and feeling your vision move up to the center of your forehead. You may experience some sort of light color there. Now breathe in for four counts, hold the breath for four counts and then breathe out for four counts. Keep this breathing going. Focus on the third eye area and let it change to whatever color it decides to. Follow this, returning to white in your head if it goes too dark or becomes black. If you don't by now feel a kind of 'pull' in that area try touching a fluorite crystal to it and leave it there for a few minutes. By now your third eye should be far more open than half an hour before and you should be ready to do your reading or to practice some techniques of divination. At this stage you can say a prayer or ask assistance from the Universe, your family guides or a higher guide. Say some thanks first though. Show gratitude for what is good in your life and then approach your divinatory tool with confidence and reverence (unless it is Rumpology!). Have an MP3 player handy to record your musings or some paper and a pen. Afterwards say a prayer of thanks. After you have finished, make sure you do the colors in reverse and gently pull the focus of energy away from your third eye back to your physical eyes. Ground yourself by imagining your feet growing roots into the floor below you. This is extremely important and should never be rushed. I have been caught out once when I didn't shut down properly and went out with my fluorite crystal still round my neck. I was rushing to pick my daughter up from work and felt very disorientated while driving. I also 'saw' a very disturbing visual of an accident that had happened on the road about six months earlier. Not pleasant! I won't forget again!

Understanding Symbols

Symbols are physical pictures that can represent something abstract or can be used to simplify a connection to a deeper event

NOW IT IS YOUR TURN!

or feeling. The Oxford dictionary says, 'a symbol is an object, idea or process that people can visualize that typifies, represents or recalls something else.' Sometimes it is easier for the brain to access one symbol than lots of little thought inputs. Symbols can have a major impact on our lives and some have very major associations. Some symbols mean one thing to one person and something very different to another. The Buddhist meaning of the swastika is very different from the energy that the Nazi swastika holds. One swastika means eternal flow and is honorable and the other is associated with fascism and racism. So, it is important that the individual be careful in interpreting symbols. What it means for you may be the total opposite of what it means to someone of another culture or spirituality.

Let's just say that you were divining for someone and a horse symbol appeared. You could interpret this as power or lust for life. However, if the person had been frightened by a horse as a child and had a phobia, then this would be a fear symbol to them. Or a pagan may view a pentagram as a spiritual blessing. Yet, a Christian may view it as a sign of witchcraft or heathenry and it then could be perceived as a threat. So it is important to be aware of certain aspects of the person when attempting a reading. If in doubt, always ask such things as 'Are you afraid of horses at all?' or 'Does this have any religious significance to you?' The inquirer won't mind as long as you explain why you are asking (that symbols are personal in interpretation).

Sometimes symbols can appear distorted or incomplete especially in reading teacups or coffee grains. So it is important to use your intuition or psychic ability to divine 'the full picture.' This will become easier with time. You will become familiar with individual symbols that mean something to you. I don't read the tarot in a basic way and sometimes can just be reading one little symbol on a particular card. If you allow yourself to become familiar with certain symbols and what they mean to you personally, then the reading will become far more accurate and precise.

This is why the dictionary of symbols that follows is simply only a guide. It is a starter pack as such for you to add on or take off, diversify and edit accordingly. It can be a good psychic tool to actually write down what certain symbols mean to you and build on it. Your higher guide or simply the Universe will give them back to you in a reading at the appropriate time. In this way you can become far more precise and accurate.

Most symbols need to be looked at in different ways. The order, the way it faces up or down, the strength of it and the alignments with other symbols are all very important. So, remember that one symbol in a moving, lucid dream can have a different meaning to a solitary symbol in tea cup. When using methods that involve fluidity or movement, such as egg readings or fire or smoke reading, make sure you watch for symbols that merge into others or that change and alter.

By simply working with your intuition and having knowledge of symbols, you will be able to work with time constraints. You can sit with a teacup and study it for hours, but the client might not be impressed. With moving forms of divination, divining must be almost instantaneous as the symbolism morphs or is lost. It may be beneficial therefore to start by reading tea leaves and then progressing to, for example, reading an egg once you have sharpened your intuition on something that does not dissipate quickly before your eyes. Otherwise you may become frustrated!

Enjoy building your knowledge of symbols and never stop learning. So many divinatory symbols are quite old-fashioned and that is why I have included objects like computers and television in the dictionary. Symbols can evolve and new ones appear once mass consciousness has caught up with modern living. Remember mainly that it is all subjective and the way you read a symbol can and will at times be very different from someone else. Be strong and learn to be confident in your own powers of prediction!

Dictionary of Symbols

Acorn
Hope for new beginnings.

Airplane
Travel. Flights of fancy. Dreams of the future. Fear. Delays.

Ambulance
Bad luck. Accidents. Be careful!

Angel
Transcendence. Protection.

Ant
Hard work ahead. Positive outcome for a group.

Apple
Good luck. A gift. Riches. With a bite out…temptation.

Apron
Secure family life.

Armor
Protect yourself.

Arrow
Take swift action. New direction. Piercing thought.

Baby
New life. Pregnancy. New business venture.

Ballerina
Need to balance responsibilities.

Balloon
Happiness. Joy.

Banana
Accidents and bad luck.

Bath
Cleanse yourself emotionally.

Bear
Success after a fight.

Bed
Sleep on issue. Rest and recovery.

Bee
Organization. Working as a team. Hard work. Transformation and success.

Beetle
Rebirth. Gathering. Recycling. Cleaning out of emotions.

Bell
Warning of trouble coming.

Belly
Vulnerability and naivety.

Bible
Question your morality.

Blood
Life force. Cleansing. Sacrifice.

Boat
Travel. Hope and optimism. Inspiration and ambition.

Book
Knowledge. Education. Communication of ideas.

Bracelet
Committed relationship and marriage.

Breasts
Nurturing and good fortune.

Bridge
A road over troubled waters. Healing of a feud. A link to your subconscious.

Broom
New directions. Leave old thoughts behind.

Candle
Guidance. Illumination. Meditation. Hope.

Car
Take control of life. Be aware of potential motions and outcomes. Travel. Slow down.

Cat
Independence. The need for personal freedom or new boundaries.

Cattle
Wealth and stability.

Chair
Rest period or time of slowing down.

Chalice
Fulfill spiritual needs. Emotional harmony.

Church
Safety or sanctuary.

Clock
Don't waste time. Timely intervention. Planning. Sometimes bereavement.

Cloud
Stormy relationship. Clouds gathering to bring a warning of a storm. Hidden actions and secrecy. Hidden good things to come.

Coat
Need for protection from outside world.

Coffin
Death of a relationship.

Coin
Money coming. Wealth and prosperity.

Compass
New horizons. Change of direction.

Computer
Be organized. Link in to memories or subconscious. Be practical and precise.

Cross
Sacrifice. Trauma. Belief. Burden. Decision making. Crossroads.

Crutch
Find support systems. Ask for help.

Dagger
Danger. Attack. Misfortune.

Death
Birth. Anxiety. New beginnings. Sometimes does predict death.

Deer
Gentle harmony. Use female instinct. Motherhood.

Diamond
Clarity. Strength. Wealth.

Dog
A guardian or guide. Family and companionship. A scary dog can mean aggression or a warning.

Door
Opportunity. New beginnings. Blockages if shut, especially sexual.

Drum
New beginnings. Make your own way in life.

Ears
Gossip. Listen carefully.

Egg
Fertility. Nourishment. Love. A pregnancy.

Eight
Destiny being fulfilled. Infinity. Long-term plans succeeding. Strength and personal power. Beware of constant intellectual weariness.

Elephant
Status. Sometimes feeling weighed down by expectations.

Eye
Need for protection. Second sight. Prophesy.

Exclamation mark
Danger. Think things out!

Feather
Freedom. Spiritual communication. Bravery. Intellect.

Feet
Ground yourself. Unwanted disputes.

Fire
Passion. Desire. Danger. Illumination. Warmth.

Flowers
A celebration. Good news coming.

Four-leafed clover
Good luck.

Fox
Cunning person. Hidden agenda.

Frog
Connection of conscious to subconscious. Revelations. News.

Glasses
Psychic vision. Second sight. Don't ignore what is on outer vision. Be aware of clouded vision.

Gold
Wealth and riches.

Gun
Be careful of violence or aggression. Act quickly.

Hair
Losing one's hair is loss of power. Cutting it is transformation or taking back control. Sometimes vanity.

Handcuffs
Feeling restrained or imprisoned.

Hands
Work to be done!

Hat
Wisdom and knowledge. Use your brain!

Heather
Good luck and good fortune.

Helicopter
Unannounced guests.

House
Stability, clan or family news. The subconscious mind. A crumbling house can mean destruction of financial security, disaster and even psychosis.

Horse
Inspiration. Lust and desire. Empathy. Strength and fortitude.

Knot
Problems ahead and much hard work to get through them.

Ladder
Progress and ambition.

Lightning
Ideas and inspiration. Fast action. Cleansing.

Lilies
Naivety. Sometimes innocence.

Lion
Strength and determination.

Lips
Being sensual or exploring sexuality. A smile is happiness and down turned lips is sadness.

Mask
Deception. Holding back on the truth.

Mirror
Reflections of oneself or subconscious. Lies or deception.

Monkey
Lies and deception.

Moon
The subconscious mind. Deception. Hidden secrets. Depression. Imagination and intuition. Fertility and ovulation.

Nakedness/nudity
Anxiety especially in place of work or on a stage.

Nest
Security. Imminent birth.

Ohm
Spirituality and inner sacredness.

Onions
Sad news. Tears.

Parachute
Safety first. Good friendship.

Poppies
Ill health. Neglect.

Phone
Communication, good or bad. Await a message. The need to communicate with someone or talk things through.

Polar bear
Isolation and loneliness.

Potatoes
Successful venture. Wealth.

Priest
Bad news is coming.

Question mark
Question your thoughts or decisions before acting.

Rabbit
Fertility. Subconscious fear. Inertia.

Ring
Completion of a cycle in life. Marriage or engagements. Invitations. Healing of a feud. Broken ring means broken promises, ending of relationships, and lack of energy for completion.

Rocks
Difficulties in way of progress.

Scorpion
The need to put self first. Self-preservation.

Shark
Survival and cunning.

Shoes
Stability and security.

Snake
Deception. Renewal. Ridding of negativity. Lust and desire. Snake climbing up means good luck. Sliding down means bad luck.

Spider
Weaving your destiny. Group consciousness. Planning and working. As a warning it can mean not to be caught in someone's web of deception.

Star
Inspiration. Destiny. Hope. Fulfillment of ambition.

Sun

Joy. Children. Good health. Optimism. Good news.

Teeth

Intact can mean a gift or good news. Falling out can be fears or insecurity.

Ties

Discipline. For females...be more assertive.

Television

Be vigilant. Watch others' actions. Watch rather than take action.

Turnip

Watch finances.

Tree

Wise guidance. Mentor. New roots. Education. Knowledge. Family and clan.

Underwear

Secrets and hidden truths.

Vampire

Emotional disharmony. Blood tests.

Veil

Seek out truth. Hidden agenda.

Zombie

Fear of death. Tiredness.

Bibliography

Books used in the Bibliomancy chapter

Amazzone, Laura. *Goddess Durga and Sacred Female Power*
Andrews, Ted. *Animal Speak*
James, E. L. *Fifty Shades of Grey*
Setiawan, Erick. *Of Bees and Mist*
Good News Bible

Web Resources

http://www.britishdowsers.org/index.shtml
http://www.buzzle.com
http://www.funonthenet.in
http://www.jacquelinestallone.com
http://www.oocities.org
http://en.wikipedia.org

Acknowledgements

Many thanks go to all at John Hunt Publishing for care and support and especially to Maria Moloney Wilbrink of Dodona for advice and guidance.

So many thanks go to my husband and daughters for their patience when maybe my mind was firmly in this book and not in the real world. Thank you for your patience. Also to Jim and Sooz for comments as the book progressed.

Also to Level 42 for being the soundtrack to my books and my inspiration through songs. Also to all my friends for support and love. You know who you are! And to my clients who are simply the best!

Many thanks to those kind people who allowed themselves to be guinea pigs for this book. You are all stars!

While I was writing these acknowledgements I felt a presence around me and felt it was my old English teacher. This lovely woman was my teacher for five years and was the main reason I was good at English. She inspired and directed me with wisdom and such a quick mind. I remember the look of horror in her eyes when I told her I was going to university to study sciences instead of my top subject of English. She said it was a wasted talent! She expected me to be a published author and I think felt a bit let down. So since she has made her presence felt today, I will include her in my acknowledgements. Thank you, Miss McElwee, your teaching wasn't wasted!

For information on what I do and also on my other books please find me on www.coletteclairvoyant.webs.com and also on Facebook as Colette Clairvoyant and Colette Brown (author).